Z215

A typical day in the life of a farm worker and his family a century ago, from the time they got up in the morning until they went to bed at night, is reconstructed here in lively and accurate detail. It is based upon a careful examination of many different nineteenth-century records, archive material, and the reminiscences of those who lived at the time. The changes seen in the countryside from the beginning of the nineteenth century to modern times are briefly surveyed in a final chapter.

The author has included a large number of photographs of relics from the period, which show in detail the objects that were to be found in farm workers' cottages at that time. There are also reproductions of a number of documents as well as pictures of farming scenes of the period.

The book will be of special value to all those interested in nineteenth-century social history, and particularly to those involved in the study of local history. An appendix describes some of the useful 'follow-up' work which may be done.

Frank Huggett has written a large number of educational books, including two on farming.

A Day in the Life of a Victorian Farm Worker

Books by the same author include:

Farming, A. & C. Black, 2nd revised edn, 1970
A Short History of Farming, Macmillan, 1970
What they've said about . . . Nineteenth Century Reformers, Oxford University Press, 1971
How it Happened, Basil Blackwell, 1971
A Day in the Life of a Victorian Factory Worker, Allen and Unwin, 1972 (uniform with this volume)

A Day in the Life of
A VICTORIAN
FARM WORKER

FRANK E. HUGGETT

LONDON · GEORGE ALLEN & UNWIN LTD
Ruskin House   Museum Street

Filmset in 12 on 13 point Baskerville and printed
Offset Litho in Great Britain by Cox & Wyman Ltd,
London, Fakenham and Reading

Contents

Illustrations

Acknowledgements

Figures 1–4, 6–11, 14–33 and 35–6 are reproduced by kind permission of the Museum of English Rural Life, University of Reading. Figure 5 is reproduced by courtesy of the Mansell Collection, and Figures 9 and 34 by courtesy of the *Land Worker* and the National Union of Agricultural and Allied Workers. We are also grateful to Miss P. E. Pemberton and the County of Hereford Record Office for permission to reproduce Figure 11, and to Mr D. L. Arkwright and the County of Hereford Record Office for Figure 13.

Preface

This book reconstructs one day in the life of a farm worker and his family a century ago, from the time they got up in the morning until they went to bed at night. It is the story of Samuel Strudwick, farm labourer; his wife, Mary, glove-maker; and their children.

Although very few farm workers have left a written record of their day-to-day life, details of how they lived are to be found in many different contemporary articles, books and reports; in archives and museums; in later reminiscences of those who lived at the time; and in modern research into the Victorian age. It is upon these sources that this account is based.

The choice of year is by no means arbitrary, for the period from 1870 to 1875 was one of the most crucial in British agriculture. It marked the end of the prosperous period of Victorian 'high' farming and, for many farmers, the beginning of a disastrous agricultural slump. The previous twenty years had been a period of great prosperity for many landowners and efficient farmers; it was anything but that for farm labourers.

Most of the book consists of a simple narrative and descriptive account of the Strudwicks' day, which is suitable for individual study or for reading in class. This is profusely illustrated with photographs of many of the objects they used in their daily lives. It is hoped that this form of illustrated story will not only bring the past alive, but will also help to stimulate the growing interest in local history in schools. Many parts of the text can be used as starting points for local investigations. Some suggestions are contained in an appendix.

Although local history can provide an excellent and exciting introduction to historical method, the results of such investigations have to be set in a wider national context if they are not to result in some distortion. The regional differences in farm workers' lives and the changes in the countryside which occurred before and after 1870 are dealt with briefly in a final chapter. This is more suitable for study by the whole class under the teacher's guidance.

There is also a list of dates, together with suggestions for further work and further reading.

1. *MORNING*

It was just after five o'clock one spring morning when Samuel Strudwick clambered out of bed. Dawn was still merely a faint glimmer on the horizon and the bedroom was illuminated only by the cold light of the moon. His wife, Mary, had got up a short time before him. Except in the depths of winter they rose at about 5 a.m. every working day. Although neither of them had a watch and there was not a clock in the house, they both knew instinctively when it was time to get up. Like the birds, which were already stirring uneasily in the eaves, they went to bed and got up early every day.

Samuel was a short, broad-shouldered man, with a fringe of whiskers around his weather-beaten face which made him look older than his forty-three years. As he got out of bed he felt aches and pains in his limbs and joints, which seemed to be getting worse every year. They were caused, he believed, by living in such a damp cottage. Some men of fifty in the village had hands which were swollen and twisted at the joints like the roots of an old tree.

It was cold and damp in the bedroom, which had no fireplace or other means of heating. The wide chimney of the large downstairs fireplace jutted out slightly from the bedroom wall. This provided a little faint heat at night, but sometimes they woke up on a winter's morning to find a layer of ice on the inside of the ill-fitting windows.

He walked quickly across the bare wooden floor to the corner of the room where his clothes were lying on an old chair. He was still wearing the shirt he had slept in. Bending down, he groped around until he found his woollen stockings and his thick corduroy trousers and put them on. Few farm workers ever wore a nightshirt or pants. After he had hitched up his trousers just below the knees with two leather straps, he put on his heavy boots, which weighed nearly 7 lb. The soles were studded all over with nails and tipped at the front and the back with iron. Inside each boot there was a layer of dried grass, which made them more comfortable to wear. Finally, he put a large red-and-white handkerchief around his neck and tucked the ends into his braces.

The bedroom was only about twelve feet long and about ten feet wide, but it was divided into two by a curtain made from bits of old blankets, frocks and bed coverings, sewn together in a random pattern like a patchwork quilt. In the other part of the room, two of his daughters—nine-year-old Naomi and five-year-old Sarah—slept together in one bed. The baby of the family, Joseph, slept beside them in a wooden cradle which all the children had used when they were younger. Most of the cottages in the village were so over-crowded that they had bedrooms divided in the same way. Some families were forced to use the downstairs kitchen as a bedroom, too. Until recently their eldest daughter, Ann, had slept in a made-up bed on the kitchen floor. But at the age of thirteen she had gone off to work as a domestic servant in London. When Naomi was a few years older, they would have to make up a bed for her in the kitchen, and if they ever had any relatives to stay that was where they would have to sleep, too.

Samuel walked across the room and into an even smaller bedroom. There was just enough room in it for a bed in which his two other sons, John and David, slept together. He went into the room and woke up the eldest boy, John, and then went on downstairs.

The narrow, creaking staircase led direct into the back kitchen, which was the same size as the smaller bedroom. It had a rather uneven floor made of rough red bricks. Scattered around the floor and on shelves, there were a number of earthenware pots and pans of various shapes and sizes. On one of the shelves there were also some knives, forks and spoons, and a few plates. There was a collection of stoneware bottles of various sizes, a wicker basket in one corner of the room and a small stack of firewood in another. His scythe, with its long wooden handle and curved blade, and his wooden rake, which he used for hay-making, rested on a few rusty nails hammered into the beams of one wall.

The back kitchen was used as a kind of store-room. The only other room was the kitchen. In this room, they cooked, ate, and sat together in the evenings. The most prominent feature of the kitchen was the large open fireplace built of brick, which stretched almost right across one wall. His wife was squatting down by the fireplace trying to coax some life into a few sticks and lumps of coal with a pair of bellows. They couldn't have afforded to buy the bellows new, but had been fortunate enough to obtain them for a few pence at a farm sale held when a local farmer had given up farming and left the district. As the fire burst into crackling flames, a couple of spiders scuttled away from the sticks towards a dark corner of the hearth.

Mrs Strudwick got up from the fireplace. She was a short, plump, rosy-cheeked woman, wearing a long thick frock, made of a mixture of wool and cotton; a long white apron, tied around her waist; and a little close-fitting cap of muslin, tied under her chin with a ribbon. She wore the cap indoors and outdoors, even when she wore her best Sunday bonnet over it. The cap kept her hair neat and tidy, and protected it from dust.

She went into the back kitchen and filled a big, black iron kettle from one of the earthenware pans on the floor. All their water had to be heated, and all their meals cooked, on the kitchen fire. She hung the kettle on the hook at the end of the iron hanger, which was fixed to a beam inside the chimney, and adjusted it so that the kettle came right down over the small fire.

Her husband opened the back door and went out. The path outside the door was wet and muddy. His heavy boots sank into the soft ground, but the straps around his legs kept the bottoms of his trousers out of the mud. Even though it was spring, it was still very cold. The weather had been no improvement on last year's. It had rained for most of January and right at the end of the month there had been heavy falls of snow which had continued into February. In March, however, there were a few warm days of sunshine, which brought the blackthorn, or sloe, into blossom before the end of the month. Samuel, who like all the other villagers studied every natural sign of what the future weather might be, knew that a cold spell would follow. It was what they called a 'blackthorn winter'.

The cold, wet weather had delayed work not only on the farm but also in his quarter-acre garden on which they depended for their supply of potatoes, cabbages, onions and other vegetables. He had been getting up very early some mornings to dig his garden by the light of the moon and had also been working in it every Sunday, his only free day. Most of it was dug now and some of it was already planted. He walked on up the garden path towards a small broken-down hut at the top of the garden which served as a privy. Inside there was a wooden seat above an open cess pit. Once a week he emptied it at night, scooping out the contents with a large ladle with a long wooden handle and transferring them into a deep trench at a far corner of the garden. Bits of vegetables, the bedroom slops and the washing water were all put in the same trench, so that when they had rotted they could be used as manure for his garden.

By the time he returned to the house, the kettle was singing. Two of his children were already up. His eldest boy, twelve-year-old John, was sitting at the table in the kitchen. Naomi, who was nine, was helping her mother to get the breakfast. She had put a few earthenware cups and basins, some plates, and a few knives and spoons on the rough wooden table. Samuel sat down on a rush-seated chair beside his son.

Breakfast never varied. Mrs Strudwick cut off two large hunks of bread from the loaf on the table, put them in basins, and sprinkled each of them with a little salt, before she poured some hot water into the basins. 'Kettle broth' was all they ever had for breakfast. At one time, they used to have bread and milk, but milk was far too expensive for them to buy now. Five years ago, his employer, Mr Bennett, had sold some of his milk locally and used the rest to make cheese and butter on the farm. But ever since the railway station had opened in the market town three miles away, he had sent practically all his milk up to London by steam train every day, keeping only enough for his own family.

While Samuel and his son were eating their breakfast, Mrs Strudwick was preparing the midday meal for them to take to work. She cut off another big hunk of bread for each of them and a slice of cheese. Then she made some weak tea in an old teapot and filled her husband's can, adding a little brown sugar. She put her husband's meal into the round wicker basket which he always took with him to the farm where he worked.

When Samuel had finished his breakfast, he got up from the table and walked over to the open fireplace. A brick had been removed to form a small gap in one corner, where he kept his clay pipes. They were all gleaming white. He had cleaned them thoroughly the previous night by putting them in the fire on his pipe rack until they came out like new. He picked out his favourite one with a small upright bowl and a short stem. A few of the younger men were now smoking briar pipes with a stem made of horn, but Samuel preferred to smoke the clay pipes he had always used because they gave a sweeter, cooler smoke. Putting on his thick fustian jacket and his billycock—or bowler—hat, he said goodbye, picked up his wicker basket and set out on his two-mile walk to work.

His son John left for work later, as he worked on a farm in the village. He had started there at the age of eight. His first job had been scaring rooks and crows away from newly planted crops by waving a large wooden rattle. Sometimes he had become so tired that he had stretched out by the hedge and fallen fast asleep until the farmer caught him. As he became older, he had gone on to other work: picking stones off fields which were to be mown; weeding turnips; and planting seeds. John had been to school for several months during the winter when there was less work to do on the farm, but he had left school altogether at the age of eleven, because the 2s 6d he earned each week was so important a part of the family budget.

Just before 5.45, John also left for work, carrying his midday meal wrapped up in a large handkerchief like the one his father wore round his neck. He was wearing an old pair of his father's trousers which had been cut down to fit him and a jacket which had been frequently patched and repaired. Like many of the village boys he was broad-shouldered, but short for his age. Naomi was slightly taller, even though she was younger, but she was rather thin and bony.

Mrs Strudwick liked to do one thing at a time, so she always tried to keep the other children in bed until her husband and her eldest boy had left for work. It wasn't too difficult to cope with them all at once in the summer, when it was light and warm in the mornings and the children could play outside the back door, but when it was too cold for that, it became impossible. The kitchen was so small that they all fell over each other's feet, she said.

Some of the more fortunate families had a wooden cradle for their babies, which was handed down from generation to generation

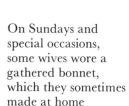

On Sundays and special occasions, some wives wore a gathered bonnet, which they sometimes made at home

Clay pipes could be
kept clean by putting
them in the fire on
a pipe rack. The coin
underneath gives
some indication of
the size

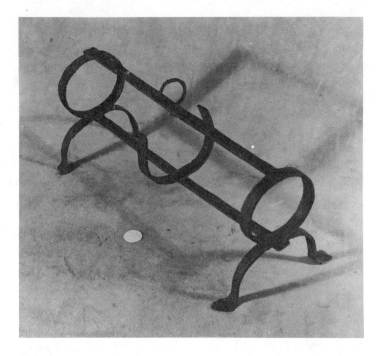

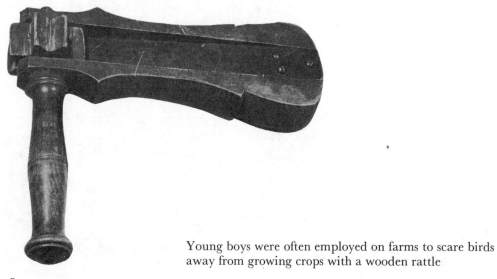

Young boys were often employed on farms to scare birds
away from growing crops with a wooden rattle

After she had called the children she started to prepare their breakfast. It didn't take her long, as their breakfast consisted only of thick slices of white bread smeared with treacle or sprinkled with sugar.

Six-year-old David came down into the kitchen first, wearing the corduroy suit that he always wore to school. His sister, Ann, had made it for him out of one of their father's old pairs of trousers just before she went off to work in London. Mrs Strudwick told him to wash his face and hands and then combed his tangled hair. Shortly afterwards five-year-old Sarah came down the stairs with her brother, Joseph, who was nearly two. Sarah wasn't starting school until the following September. Looking after her small brother was one of her main tasks: she also helped her mother in the house and had to watch the dinner bubbling in the big iron cauldron over the open fire whenever her mother was out. Sarah and Joseph were both dressed in the same way—in petticoats, frocks and pinafores.

The children sat down at the table and gobbled up their breakfast greedily. Mrs Strudwick poured out a cup of weak tea for herself and stirred in a little brown sugar. She dipped a piece of bread in the tea, ate some herself and gave some to Joseph. As soon as she had finished her scanty meal, she was up on her feet again, bustling round the kitchen. She had too much to do, and it was too cold, to sit around for long.

Meanwhile, her husband had almost completed the first half of his two-mile walk from his cottage to the Bennetts' farm, where he worked. He didn't mind the walk so much in the spring and the summer, but it was most unpleasant in the winter, particularly when it was raining or when snow lay heavily on the ground. When it was snowing he always covered his boots with a layer of melted candle grease to preserve them. But Samuel knew he was luckier than some men in the village who had to walk five or six miles to their farms and back again every day. Cottages were so scarce that most farmers could provide them on the farm itself only for the men who looked after animals—the cowman, the shepherd and the ploughman.

Samuel knew every inch of the way, for he had worked on the same farm his whole life. The lane was protected on either side by a high steep bank, spattered with little clumps of primroses and a few violets. A small bunch of primroses discarded by some child lay wilting in the mud at the foot of the bank. He walked on at a slow, deliberate pace, the legs of his corduroy trousers producing a scraping sound as they rubbed against each other and his heavy boots squelching in the mud.

As he turned out of the deeply rutted lane, he came into a slightly wider lane with a rough broken surface of flints. Every spring and summer, women and children collected stones from the fields which were then taken by wagon to the side of the lane where they were dumped in a pile. In the autumn older men who were past any other form of work broke the stones up into flints and scattered them along the lane, where the wheels of passing carts and wagons pressed them down into the mud to form a hard, but irregular, surface. The lane was exposed on either side to the cold wind blowing across the fields. Samuel stopped, as he always did every day at this point, and lit his short-stemmed clay pipe. As he puffed away at it, he could feel the warmth from the bowl glowing on his cold face comfortingly.

He trudged slowly along the lane which wound gently uphill towards the farmstead. On one side their land rose up into great rolling fields, and on the other it dropped away towards a neighbouring farmer's fields in the valley. The fields were divided by hedges and wooden fences. There was a great stillness and emptiness everywhere, with no sound but for the noise of the wind and the cawing of rooks which rose up protestingly as he passed under the tree in which their nests were built. Few strangers ever came to this area. Where the earth had just been ploughed it was brown and flinty; but where it had been planted it was blotched unevenly with the green of growing crops and many different kinds of weeds. Down below in the valley, the rough grasses of the uneven meadows were dotted with dandelions and huge clumps of dock.

From the lane he could see the farmhouse clearly, with its wisps of thin blue smoke rising from the large brick chimneystacks into the cold, clear morning air. It was a large two-storey house, facing south, with stone mullion windows and a tiled roof. In front of the house there was a pleasant garden, and on one side some rough grassland where a few apple trees were already in bud. Samuel turned into the farm track which took him round behind the house, where there was a paved courtyard enclosed by a low brick wall. At the back of the house there were two large rooms with stone floors: the brew-house and the dairy. Until recently they had both been in constant use. The brewhouse still contained the equipment for brewing beer: the great wooden casks called hogsheads which could hold more than fifty gallons of beer; the smaller brewing tubs; and the built-in copper for heating water. But they were now used only once a year for making beer for the workers in the harvest fields; it was much less trouble and almost as cheap for the farmer to buy his own beer from the local brewery.

The dairy, too, still contained some of the equipment for making butter and cheese—wooden milk pails, cream skimmers, and the big wooden cheese press—while the windows were still protected by metal gauze which had once kept marauding cats away from the ripening cream. But the dairy was now used only as a store-room and for the harvest supper once a year, while the brewhouse was used mainly by the farm workers for heating up their tea and eating their midday meal when it was too wet and cold for them to have it out in the fields.

On the other side of the track was the farmyard, with its many different buildings. Samuel passed by the old granary—a large tile-hung barn where some of the grain was stored, raised up on high brick piers to keep out the rats, and with wagons stored in the space below. A little farther on was the great barn with its oak floor where the corn had once been threshed in winter when it was impossible to do any outside work on the farm. He walked on past the cowyard towards the stables, where they all met the farmer at 6 a.m., unless they had been told previously what work they had to do that day.

Some of the men and boys had been hard at work for hours before that. By 4 a.m. a hired boy of twelve, who lived at the farm, had already started to feed, water and clean the big Shire horses which pulled the wagons, the ploughs, the harrows and other farm tools. After the head ploughman arrived at 5 a.m., he had to polish the horses' harnesses until the small brass studs in the leather gleamed and glittered in the dim light of the stables. The cowman had been up even earlier. By 3.30 a.m. he was sitting on his three-legged stool, milking the cows by the light of an old iron lantern, with panels made of horn.

Another man, the shepherd, had had scarcely any sleep at all that night, for it was the time of year when lambs were born. During the lambing season he always left his own home and lived in a small hut near the sheep, accompanied only by his constant companion, a collie dog. Even during the rest of the year he lived a hard and isolated life in his small cottage, called Shepherd's Hut, in a distant corner of the farm. He was very much his own master and the other farm workers scarcely ever saw him, except when they were sent up to help him move the hurdles, made of ash and willow, which were used when the sheep were confined to one patch of ground instead of being allowed to graze freely on the downs.

Whenever they did see him, he was invariably carrying his crook, a long staff with a curved iron end. He could catch sheep with it by hooking the end around one of the sheep's rear legs and throwing it on its back with a quick twist of his wrist. He also wore an old-fashioned garment, which had once been worn by all farm workers: a smock. It was a long, loose garment made of coarse white linen which kept out both wind and rain. It was made from two pieces of material, sewn together at the sides and gathered on the chest and the back. His best Sunday smock was elaborately embroidered.

Samuel walked on into the stables where the other farm workers and lads were already waiting. Four great Shire horses, with their short, strong legs covered from the knees down by longer white hair, like fluffy socks, stamped and pawed the ground. As they snorted, their breath could be seen on the cold morning air. Just before six o'clock Mr Bennett arrived to tell them what work he wanted them to do.

2 *AT WORK*

Some farm workers had only one room downstairs, where they had to wash, cook and eat. Notice the bread-oven on the right of the open fireplace

As the men left the stables they went their separate ways, with Mr Bennett's urgent commands still ringing in their ears. Bad weather had delayed work on the farm. There had been so much rain the previous autumn that the fields

22

were too wet for the horses to plough them, and therefore little winter wheat had been planted. Spring had also been so wet and cold that much ploughing, and planting of corn and other crops, still remained to be done. The success of the harvest rested on the speed with which they worked now and on the weather in the summer. Although more and more wheat was being imported, a good harvest was still important to them all. They depended on it for bread, their main item of food; for supplies of straw for the animals; and, ultimately, for their jobs. Samuel could remember what it had been like in the bad harvests of the 1840s when, as a lad, he had sometimes had to steal potato peelings from a pig barrel to ease his hunger. He hoped he would never see such hard times again, but you couldn't tell.

The previous autumn they had been able to plant only one small field of wheat; but there were a number of bare patches in the field, as some of the seeds had failed to germinate. Mr Bennett had told Samuel to fill in the gaps with fresh seed. He walked away from the stables, carrying his wicker meal basket, a basket of corn, and a rake over his shoulder. Two of the other men left the stables, carrying pairs of dibbling irons, to sow another field with corn. Sowing seed with dibbling irons was hard and monotonous work. You had to walk backwards across the field making two parallel lines of holes with the bulbous ends. Into each hole, a woman or a young child then dropped three grains of corn, which were covered over by a harrow pulled by a pair of horses.

When Samuel reached the cornfield, he put his wicker basket down by the hedge and walked over to the first bare patch. He raked up the weeds, scattered some seeds, and then raked the loose earth over them. Although he did not seem to work very quickly, he was so skilful at his work, that few of the other men, and none of the women, could keep up with him. The work wasn't so exhausting as some he had to do on the farm, but he was soon feeling warm, in spite of the early morning coldness. From time to time he spat upon his hands, which were dry and hard through long hours of hard work in all kinds of weather, so that he could get a good grip on the handle of the rake.

From where he was working he could see the lane leading to the farm. Strangers came into this part of the world so seldom, and he was so familiar with the limited number of animals and objects on the farm, that, like all countrymen, he could recognize people, animals and things from a great distance. So, although the lane was a considerable distance away, he was able to recognize immediately any of the villagers or any of their own cows and horses that passed along it.

Shortly before eight o'clock, he saw Polly Cook, a woman from the village, coming up the lane to work on the farm. Like most of the women she did not usually start work until 8 a.m. and left at 4 p.m., two hours before the men, so that she could get home in time to prepare her husband's dinner. Women

23

did most of the men's jobs, but were paid only tenpence a day. Samuel leaned on the handle of his rake and watched her until she was out of sight and then went on with his work methodically, pausing only now and again to watch a person, a cow, a horse and cart in the lane, to spit upon his hands, or sometimes just to stare across the fields.

Several times he saw Mr Bennett, walking along by one of the hedges. Although the farmer did not come into his field, Samuel knew that he was watching him. At different times every day, Mr Bennett would leave the job he was doing, and make a quick tour of the farm to see that everyone was doing their work properly. Samuel thought that he was a fair, but strict master. He would deduct a quarter of a day's pay if you were late for work, and he was merciless to any of the young boys or lads he found sleeping when they should have been working. But in all other ways he was a good employer, who always found his farmhands some work to do even in the wettest winter, unlike one or two of the other farmers in the district, who kept their men waiting around for two or three hours on wet days and then sent them home again—without any pay.

Mr Bennett wasn't like that. Knowing that Samuel needed the money, he often found him a little extra paid work, such as weeding, to do in the evenings, and gave him a free meal, too, before he went home. The 'missus' was good to him, too. Occasionally, she would come out from the farmhouse as he was leaving in the evening, and give him a piece of meat, such as half a sheep's head, or a few potatoes, to take home to his wife in his round basket. And if any members of his family were seriously ill, she'd call round at his cottage to see what she could do for them. Each winter she usually gave his wife a couple of old blankets or some old clothes. Samuel knew that not all farmers' wives were so helpful to their workers and their families; such help could make all the difference when your wages were so low.

His wages had been raised to 13s a week the previous year; practically all the men on other farms in the district had had a similar rise of 1s a week at the same time. Many of the men said that the farmers had put up their wages only through fear that they might go on strike as many farm labourers had done in other parts of the country. For the last year, these strikes had been one of the main topics of conversation in the village inn.

There had been nothing quite like it in the countryside for over forty years, when there had been riots all over southern England, the Midlands and East Anglia. Samuel could remember his father describing how in 1830 the sky had been reddened night after night with the flames from burning ricks, and how threshing machines had been wrecked because the farm workers thought they would put them out of a job. One man from the village had been transported to Australia for his part in the revolt; his family had never heard anything from him again.

The recent trouble had started in the Midlands. Samuel had heard all about it from other men who read the newspapers at the village inn. Just over a year ago two thousand men had held an open-air meeting by the light of lanterns one winter's night at Wellesbourne, Warwickshire. They had been addressed by a farm worker, Joseph Arch. Shortly afterwards the farmhands in that district had gone on strike for higher wages. Within a few months the movement had spread throughout the country and a National Agricultural Labourers' Union had been formed. Joseph Arch had toured the country speaking at meetings, and there had been strikes by farm workers in many different areas. There had been a meeting in the market town three miles away, but Samuel had not attended it, nor had he joined the union as some of the younger men in the district had done. He wanted nothing to do with 'foreign' agitators from Warwickshire, which was what he'd heard Mr Bennett call Joseph Arch. Of course, he'd have liked higher wages, but that wasn't the way to get them, Samuel thought. If wages went too high, the farmers would want to employ only younger, stronger men and then what would happen to him in a few years' time?

At that moment, Samuel heard the London express train whistle as it entered a tunnel near the farm. It was twelve o'clock: time for his meal. He walked over to the hedge where he had left his basket, and sat down on the ground. Taking out his food he sliced off a hunk of bread and a slice of cheese with a large, horn-handled pocket knife that he always carried with him. He put another smaller piece of bread on top of the slice of cheese and held the sandwich in his palm with his hardened, grimy thumb resting on the smaller piece of bread. From time to time he had a sip of cold weak tea. He liked to have a raw onion or two with his sandwich, but his wife hadn't been able to spare one today. Spring was always one of the most difficult times for vegetables, when the last season's store was almost exhausted and the new crops had not appeared. It was much easier in the summer when there was sometimes a glut of lettuces. At those times, Mr Bennett would allow one of the men to take some from his garden, wash them in the courtyard, and take them round to the men.

When he'd finished his meal, Samuel took out his pipe, lit it, and puffed away at it, while he watched the ploughman still hard at work in the next field. The ploughman worked from 6 a.m. to 2 p.m., with a break of half an hour for his meal, which he took earlier in the morning. During that time he walked ten miles or more and ploughed an acre of land. It was hard work and needed great skill to plough a straight furrow. If you weren't careful, you were likely to receive a heavy blow from the plough handles, as Samuel had discovered to his cost when he'd tried his hand at ploughing as a young man. He'd been bruised for weeks.

But the ploughman made it all look very simple. Samuel watched him walking with his rolling gait, somewhat like a sailor's, behind his pair of horses. One of the horses always walked on the unploughed land and the other in the furrow. Through years of practice, the latter horse acquired a dainty, pigeon-toed walk, so that he walked neatly in the middle of the furrow, without swaying or treading on the freshly ploughed earth on the other side. Samuel could hear the creaking of the harnesses and from time to time the deep-voiced commands of the ploughman, which sounded something like *wooi*, to turn left; *woot*, to turn right; *gee*, to go; and *wooa*, to stop. After he had finished ploughing at 2 p.m., the ploughman took the horses back to the stables, where they were fed and watered, cleaned and combed, and later on bedded down for the night.

Things had changed a great deal on the farm since Samuel had first started to work there for old Mr Bennett over thirty years ago. At that time, a number of farmers in the district, including old Mr Bennett, still used a pair of oxen to pull the plough; but there was only one farmer in the whole area who still used them now. One of his first jobs as a young man had been to help throw an ox over on its side and hold it down by ropes while the iron shoes were nailed to its hoofs. An occasional ox shoe was still sometimes ploughed up now. Samuel thought there was nothing to beat a pair of oxen in hilly country, though he admitted that horses could move quicker on level ground. Oxen were stronger than horses, too, and they were still sometimes called in to pull a heavy load out of the mud when the horses could do nothing but dash against their harnesses without effect.

At one o'clock, Samuel put away his pipe, picked up his rake, and went back into the field. The weather was a little more pleasant now. The wind had dropped and the sun had come out, but there was still a touch of coolness in the air, and Samuel was pleased to be starting work again. He had a great interest in his farm and took a great pride in his work. He worked on at the same steady pace, pausing now and again as some sight or sound attracted his attention. Much of his work was solitary—hedging and ditching, spreading manure, hoeing. Even when he was working with others, he was often silent. The long hours of tiring labour and the ever-watchful eyes of his master gave little scope for lengthy conversations. His was a hard job, but it had great compensations. He felt himself to be part of the farm; he liked working in the open air; and you could do any job in your own way, so long as the results were satisfactory. There was no other job he would have liked instead. The worst thing of all, he thought, must be to work in a factory. Some of the younger men had already left the village to work in a factory in a town. Samuel couldn't understand how they could be happy working at the same job in the same place day after day, even though their wages were much higher than his.

The changing seasons of the year gave his work a great variety. Summer

Hay, and in some parts of the country corn, too, was cut by a team of mowers with their long-handled scythes. Notice the hazel twig attached to the foot of the shaft in the shape of a bow, which helped to keep the hay flat so that it was easier to handle

27

During the harvest, the farmer provided free beer or cider for his workers. It was drunk from little wooden kegs, called harvest bottles, which were often inscribed with the owner's initials

Mugs were made from the horn of a bullock, which was scraped and polished until it was smooth

was the busiest season of the year. First of all, there was hay-making. By early morning he would be hard at work in the hayfield, the sharp, curved blade of his long-handled scythe sweeping through the grass. He usually led the team of four or five other men, who worked in an oblique row behind him. Samuel kept up a steady pace which all the other men had to maintain. From time to time, he would stop to sharpen the blade of his scythe on a strickle, a piece of wood with fine sand embedded in adhesive material on one side. The other men would all stop to sharpen their scythes, too, when the field would ring with the sound of music, for each scythe gave out a slightly different note as it was rubbed. After the grass had been pitched into haycocks to dry, it was taken by wagon to the farmyard, where it was built into large ricks, which were then thatched.

But the biggest job of the whole year was the harvest, which usually went on for a month. It was also the most profitable, as he got extra pay which almost covered his year's rent. Every available man, woman and child in the village was employed on the harvest. Even so, there was still too much work for them to do alone, and Mr Bennett had to employ some Irishmen, who travelled around the country helping with the harvest. They were paid 5s, or more, a day—plus free beer—and at night they slept in the barns or sometimes under the hedges.

They all started work in the field as soon as the dew had evaporated from the corn, cutting it close to the ground with a heavy, short-handled hook. A couple of women, or a woman and a child, worked with each reaper, tying the corn with three or four stalks into a small bundle called a sheaf. Eight or ten of these sheaves were then rested against each other so that they stood upright and could dry out in the wind and the sun. The sheaves had to be turned every day or so to make sure that all the corn dried thoroughly. When it was all completely dried out, it was loaded with a two-pronged pitchfork on to a farm wagon and carted off to the farmyard where it was stored, or built into a haystack. One or two of the bigger farmers in the district used a mechanical reaper, drawn by a pair of horses, to cut their corn. But Mr Bennett hadn't much faith in those machines; he thought they didn't work very well with corn which had been bent and twisted by heavy storms. Samuel, however, had once heard him say that if the Irishmen kept on demanding higher wages, he'd have to buy a machine and use that instead.

During the harvest, work continued until late at night when the big red harvest moon was often hanging low over the busy fields. It was thirsty work and Mr Bennett provided them with weak beer made in the brewery at the farm. The men carried it out into the fields in wooden harvest bottles—small oak barrels with handles made of rope or plaited horse hair. Some of them held a gallon of beer. Samuel thought there was nothing more refreshing during the rest-breaks than to hold the wooden bottle above his head and let the beer stream down into his mouth from the projecting mouthpiece. At intervals during the day, fresh supplies of beer were brought out into the fields in large stoneware bottles with a curved handle on the neck.

The work was hard and exhausting under the hot sun. By the end of the day the sweat and the dust from the reaped corn had combined to cake on their bodies into a thick layer of dried dust. After they had finished work, some of the lads and the younger men liked to go off to the river for a 'bath', but Samuel preferred to wash himself down under the pump in the courtyard.

When the last wagonload of corn had been brought in from the fields, the most exciting event of the whole harvest, if not of the whole year, took place. All the men, women and children who had taken part in the harvest, plus one or two of the village craftsmen, like the blacksmith, the thatcher, and the wheelwright, sat down together at a long table in Mr Bennett's old dairy. He himself sat at the head of the table, and his wife sat at the other end. There were flowers on the table and flags hung from the beams in the roof. The farm workers had their best meal of the year—roast beef, a side of mutton, and vegetables, followed by plum pudding. In front of each person there was a horn mug, made from a section of bull's horn which had been scraped clean and polished and then fitted with a flat disc of horn at the bottom. There was as much home-brewed beer to drink as anyone wished.

After the meal clay pipes and tobacco were placed upon the table. Some toasts were drunk and then three men stood up, each holding a horn mug of beer. One of them sang a song, whose words they all knew by heart:

> Here's a health unto our master, the founder of the feast,
> I hope to God with all my heart his soul in heaven may rest,
> And all his works may prosper that e'er he takes in hand,
> For we are all his servants, and all at his command—
> So drink, boys, drink, and see you do not spill,
> For if you do you shall drink two, for 'tis our master's will.

Any of the three men who spilt a single drop of beer, immediately had his mug refilled. By that time everyone was becoming fairly merry. The women and the children were all sent home and shortly afterwards Mr and Mrs Bennett also left. The men continued with their drinking, singing, and joking until it was past midnight.

The harvest supper was one of the highlights of the year, but there was no respite in their round of toil, which continued the following day as usual. Many of the men did not go home that night, but lay down in the dairy or a barn, so that they would be ready for work again at six o'clock the following morning. Sundays and Christmas Days were their only holidays, though Mr Bennett always allowed any man who wished to do so to attend the church service in the village on Good Friday morning.

No other period of the year brought such great activity and so much excitement as the summer. In autumn the potatoes had to be lifted; beans, clover and wheat had to be sown; and weeding had to be done. Winter, with its rain, snow and ice, was the bleakest season of the year, when the cold, damp cottages were cheerless in the short evenings. The main jobs on the farm were making manure heaps, building stables, and threshing the corn to separate the grains from the stalks.

Until quite recently all threshing had been done by hand on Mr Bennett's farm. It had been one of Samuel's main occupations in the winter. Day after day he had worked with his flail, a wooden rod joined to a thinner wooden handle by an iron ring and a piece of leather, swinging it over his shoulder and bringing it down sharply on the stalks of corn on the oak floor of the great barn. It had been one of the most boring jobs of the whole year, just what it must be like to work in a factory, Samuel always thought. But none of them had to do this work any more. All the corn was threshed by a steam-powered machine which Mr Bennett hired from the local innkeeper.

At that moment Samuel heard the harmonious tinkle of some bells coming from the lane. He recognized the sound immediately; it was coming from one of their own wagons. Whenever a wagon was taken into the lanes, a set of latten bells was fixed into the horses' collars. There were three or four bells in each set, designed to ring in harmony; each set gave a slightly different sound. They were used to warn other carters of the wagon's approach, so that they could wait in a lay-by of the narrow lane until the wagon had passed.

Joseph Arch, who founded the first national trade union for farm workers, travelled to all parts of the country to attend meetings. This early photograph was taken at Yeovil, Somerset

The ploughman was one of the most important workers on the farm. This photograph of a Norfolk-type plough was taken in about 1880

Samuel looked up as the wagon came up the farm track. He could see the weak sunlight glinting on the ornamental brasses of the horses' harnesses. These were worn whenever the horses went outside the farm. The assistant ploughman was walking on one side, carrying his whip with its brass-ringed handle in his hand. On the other side there was a young lad, who helped him to load and unload the wagon and put on the brakes when the horses were going downhill. Samuel could tell by the position of the sun in the sky that it must be almost six o'clock. Another day's work was nearly over. He scattered a few more seeds, raked them in, and then walked over to the hedge to get his wicker basket before he started on his walk home.

3. AT SCHOOL

Earlier that morning two of Samuel's children, Naomi and David, had left home just before eight o'clock to walk the two and a half miles to the school in the next village. Naomi was carrying their weekly school fees of fourpence tied up in a red-and-black handkerchief, which also contained the two pieces of bread they would have for their midday meal.

They walked side by side down the narrow, muddy lane which led into their village. Naomi was wearing a frock made of coarse wool and cotton, and a long white pinafore, while David was wearing his corduroy suit. Despite the differences in their age and sex, there were some similarities in their appearance. They both wore boots; they both had small round hats made of black felt; and they both had their hair cut short, though Naomi would have liked to have worn hers long as some of the other girls did in her class at school. Mrs Strudwick usually cut their hair for them with the large pair of iron scissors which she also used for cutting out clothes. But she would send them to Granny Goodman for a haircut before special occasions, such as the Sunday school treat in July—when all the children attended a service in church followed by a free tea of fruit pies and tarts. Granny Goodman was a very old, thin woman, dressed invariably in a long white apron, a black shawl pinned over her shoulders, and a white, frilly cap. She made a few pence each week by cutting hair.

Naomi and David walked through the village and stopped for a little while to stare silently at some men unloading bricks from a wagon for the new school which was just being built in their village. They walked on towards the forge and stopped again to watch the blacksmith, in his leather apron, hard at work over his anvil, and then continued until they reached the lane which led into the next village. Fields stretched away on either side, giving no protection from wind or rain, so that it sometimes felt cold even on an early summer's morning. They ran along together, splashing their legs with mud as they slipped in the deep, water-filled ruts made by wagons. After they had run and walked for about a mile and a half, they turned off the lane and climbed over an old oak stile, whose top bar had been polished smooth by constant use. A footpath led to a small bridge over a shallow stream, where otters could sometimes be seen, and on into the next village.

Naomi thought they might be late, so she tugged at her brother's hand to make him hurry, slowing down again only when she could see the top of the church tower rising up above the trees. At that moment they heard the school bell ringing, warning them that there were only five minutes left before the school doors would be closed and locked. They hurried along the path again.

The footpath came out by the church. They opened a gate and followed several boys and girls through the churchyard, past a freshly dug grave covered with flowers, towards the rectory.

The schoolroom had been provided about twenty years before by the squire and a few other rich farmers in the village. It stood near the great tithe barn at the rear of the rectory, where in the past the rectors had stored their share of the corn that all the farmers had been obliged to give them after the harvest. The schoolroom was built of red bricks, decorated with a pattern of black bricks round the small windows. It had a tile let into the wall which read, 'We train them for Heaven'.

Naomi, David and the other children walked through the stone porchway into a small cloakroom, with a few nails on the walls, where children who had

The religious element was strong in nineteenth-century education. The tile let into the wall of this school reads 'We train them for Heaven'

34

cloaks or coats could leave them. One of the older boys, a twelve-year-old monitor, who was paid 1s a week for looking after the younger pupils, was standing on the left-hand side. On the other side, the pupil-teacher, who was a year older, was pulling the rope that tolled the school bell. The children walked past them into the schoolroom which felt cold and damp as the stove was lit only in the winter.

The oblong schoolroom had a high ceiling containing two large ventilators. It was severely furnished. The walls were bare and whitewashed to reflect the dim light which entered through the diamond-shaped panes of the small windows. At one end of the room, there were two cupboards in which the books, pens and penholders, ink and paper, chalk, and sewing materials were stored. Against the two longest walls, there were parallel rows of wooden desks with iron legs, facing outwards into the room. The far end of the room was taken up entirely by the gallery, a series of deep, wide steps which rose up in tiers from the floor almost to the ceiling.

The children clattered across the room towards the gallery and clambered up the steps to their appointed rows. David took up his place in the bottom row, while Naomi went to the one above him. The children were arranged according to their ages and their abilities. The infants of four to seven occupied the bottom row, which was always fairly full, as many mothers, particularly those who were working on farms, were only too glad to send their young children to school. But the higher the row, the fewer the number of pupils, so that the top row was occupied by only a handful of children of twelve or thirteen. Most children had left school by then. Many of the children who should have been at school did not come. It was very rare for more than half of the whole school to be present at the same time. In summer, many of the children stayed away to pick fruit or to help with other work on the farms. In the autumn, some helped with potato picking or acted as beaters in the fields and woods, scaring out the pheasants and the partridges for the squire and his friends to shoot. In winter, many children were always ill and others stayed away because they had no boots. At all times of the year the schoolmistress received many different excuses: one child had stayed away to help her mother; another to watch a funeral; another to attend a fair.

The school bell stopped ringing and the monitor locked the door. The schoolmistress, wearing a long black dress, walked over to the gallery, while the monitor and the pupil-teacher came and stood on either side of her. After they had sung a hymn and said a prayer, the schoolmistress read them a passage from the Bible. Then all the children, except the infants, scrambled down from the gallery and sat down on the wooden benches behind the desks, six of them to each desk. The monitor and the pupil-teacher took charge of them while they waited for the schoolmistress to mark the register.

The village school. A photograph taken in the 1870s in Oxfordshire

She started with the infants, occasionally turning round to glare at a class which was making too much noise.

That day the registration took longer as the school fees had to be collected. Many of the children had failed to bring their twopence, and the school-mistress had to make a note of their names so that she could send a bill to their parents. When all the registers had been marked and the fees collected, the school door was unlocked. By that time, most of the latecomers had dis-appeared, but those who had waited came in and were scolded by the schoolmistress for being late.

At ten o'clock the lessons started. They were more or less the same every day. The first period in Naomi's class was devoted to writing. The pupil-teacher told them to take out their slates and their slate pencils which were lying on a shelf below the desk. Before they started, they all had to take up their writing positions. The pupil-teacher told them to sit up straight at their desks, with the end of their tin pencil holders pointing at their right shoulders and the left elbows resting on the desk immediately in front of their left shoulders. After the pupil-teacher had written a few capital letters and a few small letters on the blackboard in copperplate writing, they had to copy them over and over again on their slates for half an hour.

In the centre of the room the schoolmistress was taking an older class in reading, which they did standing to attention; and at the far end of the room the infants were chanting short sentences from their reading books. They knew every word by heart:

Is it a bat? No! It is a fat ox. Let me pat the ox. Is he to hit the cat? No, he is not to hit the cat, or the kit. Do not put the kit in the hot pit. Let the cat get the rat. My nut is in my hat, but the hat is not in the hut. A rat is in the hut. Put the nut on the mat, but do not put the pot on the mat. Let Pat cut a bit of fat, but not the fat of the ox. Do not get in a pet, but pat the kit on the mat. My hat is so wet. Sit on a sod and nod to me. A cat sits on a sod and nods to a lad. Am I to sit on a sod? No!

In spite of the earlier coldness the room was already becoming stuffy and overheated. The warmth and the unending chant from the infants' gallery was making Naomi feel drowsy and she was pleased when the pupil-teacher told them to take their slates to the centre of the room for drill arithmetic. They all had to stand in a straight line down the room. The schoolmistress gave them a simple sum to do. The first one to finish took his or her slate up to the schoolmistress. If they had the right answer, they started a new line on her right; but if they were wrong, they went to the head of a new line on her left. There was always great competition to finish first and it soon seemed time for the morning break.

37

Mr Thurston

pleas to
excuse Deima
she as a bad
knee
yours &
S Gurney

Jany 21 94
Jas Breece
Pinmorehill

Mr Matto
Hope School
Sir the Doctor said
That i wos not to send
George to school before
But e is all right now
& i hope e will continuea
So hoping yours mrs
is mush better
yours Truetey
James Breece

These two pairs of letters from Herefordshire parents and their children show the improvement in handwriting and spelling brought about by education. The children's letters were doubtless dictated or copied

Hope School
March 18th 1878.

Honoured Sir

I am now in my 14th year, and my parents think I ought to go to work, as I am a big, strong, boy. With your kind permission therefore they would like me to leave School about May.

I beg to remain,

Honoured Sir,

Your very humble servant,

George Preece.

J. H. Arkwright Esqre

Hope School
Aug. 9th 1889

Honoured Madam

I am now leaving school, and wish to thank you for all your great kindness to me, and for my free education.

I am
your humble servant
Decima Gurney.

All the children went out into the playground, which was just a small square patch of earth, baked into hard, dried mud in the summer months, but wet and muddy for much of the rest of the year. Some of the girls played rhyming games in a circle, while some of the boys played chuck-halfpenny by throwing metal buttons torn off old soldiers' uniforms at a hole in the ground. The bell soon rang for them to go in again.

It was now the turn of Naomi's class to practise reading in the middle of the schoolroom. They all stood to attention in a straight line, with their toes against a line chalked on the floor by the monitor. The schoolmistress gave each pair a reading book. It was a rather dull-looking book with an engraved title on the front of the black cover. There were a few small illustrations in the book. They all turned to the same story they had read many times before, called 'The Idle Boy'. Some of them could chant their way through it almost without bothering to look at the book. After they had read through it together, the schoolmistress told a number of them to read one or two sentences aloud.

Before long, school was dismissed. They went into the playground again and gnawed at their slices of bread. In summer, a few of the more fortunate children also brought an apple.

The school bell rang again at 1.30. After the registers had been marked, the boys did arithmetic, while the girls did needlework. They took their sewing materials out of one of the cupboards and sat down at their desks. On Friday afternoons the ladies' sewing committee always came to inspect the work that had been done during the week.

They had not been sewing for very long before three ladies, headed by the rector's wife, came into the schoolroom. They wore bonnets and long silk dresses, and one of them carried a fan which she flickered constantly just in front of her nose. The girls had to repair pillow cases and sheets, and to hem shirts and gowns. If their work did not meet with the approval of any member of the ladies' committee, which frequently happened, they had to unpick it and start all over again. Most of the work came from the rector's wife, who had a large family. Needlework was considered to be one of the most important subjects, as it could help to gain a girl a good job as a domestic servant in the town. They had needlework for nearly one and a half hours each day.

After the afternoon break in the playground, they returned to the school-room for the last lesson, which was always singing. They all trooped into the gallery again. At that moment the rector came in. The whole school stood to attention and the schoolmistress curtsied. Although the rector often visited the school, it was unusual for him to come on a Friday afternoon. He told them that an inspector was coming to visit the school on Tuesday, and that they all had to be punctual, clean and neatly dressed. Finally, he announced that the squire had again agreed to give an orange to every boy and girl who attended school on that day.

Pattens were worn by countrywomen to keep their
shoes out of the mud

Brooms were made of
bundles of birch twigs

China ornaments,
such as this one of
Queen Victoria,
were very popular.
Collectors now pay
high prices for these
Staffordshire figures

Large iron doorkeys
are still used in many
country cottages
to this day

An inspector visited the school each year to examine the children in a number of different standards, ranging from I to VI, though no one in that school had ever got beyond Standard IV. Naomi had failed Standard I last year and had to take it again. She could still remember what had happened last time.

They had had to stand in two lines in the middle of the schoolroom, back to back to prevent cheating, with their slates and pencils in their hands. The inspector had dictated a few letters and numbers, which they had had to write down on their slates. After he had collected the slates, he heard each of them read a few sentences from a book.

The examination of the lower standards did not last long. After the children had been examined they were sent home clutching the squire's orange, which was given to them by the pupil-teacher from a basket in the cloakroom. The inspector then examined the small number of candidates for Standard IV.

Each of these candidates sat down at a desk and was given half a sheet of paper and a pen and ink. They had to write a simple sentence, such as 'I am grateful for all the benefits which I receive' which was dictated to them by the inspector, and then to do two sums, such as the following:

I can go to a certain town by the railway in 9 hours, 25 minutes and 30 seconds; it would take me at least five times as long to go by the stage coach. How long would the coach take?

Two vessels sailed for America. One of them was 9 weeks, 6 days and 14 hours on the voyage; the other got to America in 7 weeks, 5 days and 19 hours. What was the difference in time they took to make the voyage?

Finally, each of them had to read aloud a short passage from Dickens, Thackeray or Bacon, or part of a poem by Shelley, Pope or Wordsworth. The inspector had usually finished his work before lunchtime.

After the rector had made his announcement, they all sang a few songs. There was a final prayer and the school was dismissed at four o'clock. Naomi and her brother set out on their long walk home.

4. AT HOME

Some time before Naomi and David left for school, Mrs Strudwick had started her main domestic task of the day. They had so little to eat and the daily variation in their diet was so small that cooking occupied little of her time. But with her large family washing, ironing, patching and mending the clothes took up several hours of her day. Once a week she boiled some of the clothes in the big iron cauldron in which she also cooked their meals. She did the rest of the washing just outside the back door, unless it was raining or bitterly cold when she did it in the back kitchen.

There was no running water, and not even a sink, in the house. Every drop of water had to be fetched from the well by the side of the house. Mrs Strudwick was luckier than some of the other women in the village. Many of them had no well of their own, but had to share one with six or more other families. A few families, who had no well to use at all, collected what rainwater they could in an old barrel outside the back door, or took their pails to the little brook which ran through the village. In summer when the brook and the wells sometimes ran dry, they were all forced to rely on two or three old men and women who walked into the market town, returning with two pails of water suspended by chains from a wooden yoke over their shoulders, which they sold for $\frac{1}{2}$d a pail. Or they had to make the journey into town themselves.

Mrs Strudwick went into the back kitchen and lifted the wooden covers off the large, brown earthenware pans in which the water was stored. They were almost empty. Normally, her husband filled up the pans every night, but he had been getting up so early to dig the garden that he hadn't done it for the past few weeks. Mrs Strudwick picked up a wooden pail made of thick staves of seasoned oak bound together with wide iron hoops. Outside the back door she paused to put on her pair of pattens, thick wooden soles with an iron ring underneath, which kept her boots out of the mud. Although they were a little difficult to walk on, most women in the village wore their pattens when they went out into the garden or into the muddy lanes, which were always marked with the circular impressions of the pattens' iron hoops.

The mud was deep around the well where the earth was always moist. Mrs Strudwick fixed her pail to the iron hook and lowered it into the well until the pail plopped into the water below. She turned the windlass and heard the pail clanking against the sides of the well as it came towards the surface.

As she took the heavy pail off the hook, she stumbled on her clumsy pattens and had to catch hold of the wooden structure above the well to prevent herself from falling. At one time she had always taken her baby boy, Joseph, with her to the well, but she had stopped doing so ever since one of the village children had fallen down a well and been drowned.

She carried the pail of water back to the cottage. After she had washed the clothes in a wide, red earthenware pan on a table outside the back door, and had wrung them out, she didn't throw the water away. Instead, she carried the pan up the garden and tipped the soapy water into the trench, where the chamber pots and the privy were also emptied, to help the contents rot down into manure for the garden. Farm workers couldn't afford to throw away any waste material, but always tried to find some use for it. Potato peelings, for example, were particularly valuable. They could be put in the manure trench; they could be dried at the back of the fire and burnt to save coal; or they could be put into the pig barrel by the back gate, which was emptied once a week by Willy East, a villager who kept his own pig. Whenever he killed a pig he brought round a small piece of lights or the liver to all the cottagers who had helped to feed it.

Mrs Strudwick came back down the garden path, holding the empty pan in her hand. She picked up the wicker basket of chemises, drawers, shirts and petticoats and took it indoors. She didn't have a clothes line in the garden as she'd found that the hemp line rotted in the winter and snapped in the summer if it was left outside. When the weather was particularly fine she draped the clothes over the bushes in the garden to dry them; at other times she dried them on a line stretched across the back kitchen. After she had hung her washing on the line indoors, she started her housework. The house was so sparsely furnished that it wasn't a very difficult task.

From the outside her cottage home looked very pretty, especially in the summer when almost the whole of the back wall was covered with the yellow blooms of a large rambling rose, which trailed round the back door and over the window. Near the back door there were several sweet-smelling bushes of lavender and southernwood, and just beyond them a twisted old apple tree. In front of the house, which was built of big blocks of old grey stone, there was another, smaller garden with more rose bushes and other flowers—hollyhocks, columbine and sweet peas. In the summer sunshine when the bees were droning among the flowers and the many-coloured butterflies were flitting from bush to bush no dwelling could have looked more delightful—from the outside.

But the interior was anything but that. Like most of the cottages in the village it had only four rooms—two upstairs and two downstairs. All the walls were uneven and the ceilings were low. The small windows admitted little light, but a great deal of air, particularly in the winter, because the leaden frames were so bent that they did not fit securely into the rotted wooden window-frames. The heavy oak doors, which hung on big iron hinges, were warped by damp and also created many draughts. The downstairs floors were paved with brick, and as there was no damp course, the walls and the floors were usually wet in winter.

The rent was so low, only 1s 6d a week, that the landlord, who owned several other cottages in the village, rarely did any repairs and never made improvements. Even though their cottage was cold, damp, dark and draughty, there were a number in the village which were even worse. Their broken windows were stuffed up with pieces of sacking and rags; there was green fungus on some of the walls. Those with thatched roofs were often among the worst. Although a thatched roof kept the cottage cool in summer and warmer in winter, birds soon tore the thatch apart to build their nests, so that the roof leaked unless it was kept in good repair.

Mrs Strudwick went into the kitchen to start her housework. She told Sarah to take Joseph into the back garden while she tidied up. The only furniture in the kitchen was a rough wooden table; four straight-backed chairs with wicker seats; an old three-legged milking stool and a couple of blocks of wood, on which the younger children sat; a box in which she kept her sewing; an iron cauldron and a kettle near the fire; and a hearthrug which she had made from rags herself. Above the fireplace there was a wooden mantelpiece on which stood two candlesticks, which could also be used to hold a rushlight, and a few cracked china ornaments of a cat, a dog, and the Queen. Her most prized possession also stood there: a broken Toby jug which Mrs Bennett had given to her. The only other decoration in the room was a picture of an octopus, torn out of a copy of the *Family Friend*, which had been given to Ann by the rector when she was still at school. It was nailed to a wooden beam above a shelf, and had now become a little grimed and yellowed with age. On the shelf lay their only book—a leather-bound Bible. Inside the front cover the names and the birthdates of all her children had been written, including that of the boy who had died of whooping cough when he was six months' old.

Mrs Strudwick shook the rag rug out of one of the windows and laid it on a chair. Then she took the birch broom down from the two large rusty nails on which it rested above the mantelpiece. She bought all her brooms—which were made of birch twigs bound to a rough wooden handle by thin strips of hazel—from a broom-maker in the woods, for threepence each. The brick floor of the kitchen was covered with a fine layer of sand, which she renewed every Saturday after she had washed the floor on her hands and knees. Mrs Strudwick thought the sand kept the floor dry and clean. She swept carefully around the room, drawing the sand into large, swirling S-shaped patterns and then put the rug back in front of the fireplace.

After she had swept the back kitchen and tidied it, she told Sarah to look after Joseph while she went into the village to see if she could buy a loaf of bread. Leaving her two children in the house, she locked the back door with its big iron key, but left the key in the lock as she always did when she was going to be away from home for only a short time. She put on her pattens again and went along the lane towards the village. Like most of the women in the village she wore the same clothes indoors and outdoors—a thick frock, an apron, a close-fitting muslin cap, and when it was cold, a black shawl.

Normally she bought all her bread in the market town three miles away, carrying it back in a large wicker basket or tied up in her apron or in a large handkerchief. But she had too much to do that day to go all the way into town. She hoped she would be able to buy a loaf of bread from one of the women in the village. Very few of them now baked their own bread, even if they had a bread-oven, but one or two of the older women still did so.

When she reached the first cottage in the village she found Mrs Stevens just baking some fresh loaves. Mrs Stevens was fortunate enough to have a bread-oven built into the thick brick wall of the open fireplace in her kitchen. She was just scraping out the ashes of the burnt twigs and gorse from the six-foot-deep bread-oven. Mrs Strudwick watched her as she put the loaves into the hot oven with a long-handled shovel called a peel. She always made cottage loaves so that two loaves could be baked in the space of one. When all the loaves had been put in, she closed the iron door. It would not be opened again until the loaves were ready to come out, all hot and crisp, with pieces of charcoal sticking to the bottom, which many people thought made them even more tasty. Mrs Stevens still had a loaf to spare from last week's baking, and after they had chatted for a while, Mrs Strudwick left to return home.

Back in her own cottage, she settled down to her sewing. She made a few shillings each week by sewing gloves for a factory in the market town. She collected the cut-out skins each week and had to stitch them together, finish them, and make the buttonholes. She made them on a glover's donkey, a little wooden stand with a metal vice at the top which held the two sides of the gloves together. It took her two hours or more to make a pair of gloves and she made fifteen pairs every week for which she was paid 3s 6d.

It was laborious work and could be unprofitable if you were not very careful, as you could be fined for spoiling the skin if you made a serious mistake, and if the stitching was not perfect, they would try to give you a lower price. But she preferred to do this work at home, rather than work on a farm as some other women did, picking stones off the fields, hoeing, carting and spreading manure, and pulling out couch grass for tenpence a day. She did not like to leave her two youngest children locked up alone all day in the house, with nothing to eat but a crust of dry bread.

The only time she ever helped on the farm was in the harvest, when the weather was fine and she could take her two children with her and let them play around with the other children by the hedge. She wasn't very fond of farm work; she'd had too much of it as a child. Every year, from a very early age, she'd had to go gleaning with her mother, picking up the loose ears of corn in the fields after the harvest had been gathered. When it had been threshed, they'd taken it to the miller who had ground it into flour for a few pence. Some of the women in the village went gleaning, but Mrs Strudwick did not go with them.

She hadn't finished her weekly quota of fifteen gloves yet, and she bent over the wooden donkey, working quietly but swiftly in the dim light.

5. AFTERNOON

By the afternoon the sun was shining, and it felt a little less cold. Mrs Strudwick opened the front door as she always did when the weather was fine: it helped to dry out the house and let more light into the low-ceilinged room. Sarah had gone along the lane to try to find a few sticks for the fire. Joseph was playing by her feet with a bunch of rags which she'd sewn into the rough shape of a doll.

Her children had to make all their own amusements. They played games such as leapfrog and hopscotch and sometimes, after the harvest, they had the pleasure of playing on a rough seesaw in the farmyard. But they had very few toys. A home-made rag doll, a monkey on a stick bought at the local fair, and a windmill on a stick given to them by the rag-and-bone man were all the toys any of her children had ever had. The thatcher had once given Naomi a little straw effigy of a bird, like the 'dolly' he attached to some of the houses he thatched, but it had been torn apart long ago.

When Sarah returned, Mrs Strudwick went out into the garden again. She pulled up one of the few remaining cabbages and brought it back to the house. After she had cut it up and washed it, she peeled a few potatoes, adding these vegetables to the remainder of the previous day's stew in the big, black three-legged cauldron. They rarely had meat on Friday, because all of her week's money had usually gone by then.

Friday's dinner was the most scanty of the week, though the others were not much better. There was a monotonous regularity about all their meals. Dinner was their main meal of the day. Nearly every night it consisted of a small piece of bacon or pork, plus whatever vegetables were available from the garden—potatoes, cabbage, onions, turnips. The bacon was fat and the pork was pickled, and all the stews were greasy. Those two kinds of meat were not only cheap but also economical, as they did not shrink much when they were cooked and could be easily cut into small pieces.

The main variation in their diet came on Saturdays when Mrs Strudwick walked into the market town to take in her finished gloves and to pick up the new skins for the following week. She always did her shopping at the same time. Out of the money she received for making the gloves she always bought a little 'treat'; a piece of black pudding, some faggots, or some salt herrings. Occasionally, Willy East would bring her a piece of liver or lights from a pig he'd just killed. And sometimes, Mrs Bennett would give them a piece of cow's head or half a sheep's head. Apart from the harvest supper, their best meal of the year came on Christmas Day when Mrs Strudwick always tried to buy a joint of cheap mutton to roast. As she had no roasting spit, she would hang it from a chain above the fire, or if it was particularly good she would take it to Mrs Stevens in the village and pay her a penny to roast it with her own Christmas joint.

Their chief food was bread: every day they ate a 4 lb. loaf which cost 8d. It was very rare for them to have butter as it cost 1s 8d a pound. Instead she bought $\frac{1}{2}$ lb. of treacle every week, which cost only 3d a pound, and spread it on the children's bread for breakfast and tea, or sprinkled the bread with brown sugar when the treacle had run out. She bought $1\frac{1}{2}$ lb. of sugar every week at 6d a pound, which she used mainly for sweetening tea. Another expensive item was the tea itself, which cost 1s a quarter, so she bought only 2 ounces a week. Each week she bought 3 lb. of the cheapest meat at 8d a pound and 1 lb. of cheese for 4d. They burned 1 cwt of coal a week, which cost 1s. If she'd been able to burn more wood, she could have saved money, but some of the local farmers would not give you permission to pick up branches and twigs from their fields, even after they'd been blown down in a storm. Soap cost her $2\frac{1}{2}$d a week, and in winter she spent 5d a week on a pound of candles. The rent was 1s 6d a week, and school fees 4d.

Her weekly budget for these bare necessities was:

	s	d
Bread	4	8
Treacle		$1\frac{1}{2}$
Sugar		9
Tea		6
Meat	2	0
Cheese		4
Coal	1	0
Soap		$2\frac{1}{2}$
Eight candles		5
Rent	1	6
School fees		4
	11	10

This left only 1s 2d a week out of her husband's wages of 13s. Her husband smoked two ounces of tobacco a week, which cost 4d. His fees for the village benefit club were 1s a month. He had to provide his own scythe, which cost

7s 6d, his own bagging hook for cutting corn, which cost 3s, and other tools, and also had to have them repaired when necessary by the village blacksmith. Then there were all the items she had to buy from time to time such as salt, sand for the floor, plates, mugs and basins, and many other things. One of the most expensive items in her budget was clothing, particularly boots which cost 15s a pair and usually had to be renewed each year. She made all the clothes she could at home, except for her own best bonnet, some of her children's Sunday clothes, and her husband's best suit which he bought in the market town. The last one had cost £3 6s.

Most weeks she didn't know how to make ends meet, and would never have been able to do so, but for her husband's extra earnings in the harvest, and the few extra shillings that she earned every week by making gloves and those that her eldest boy, John, earned by working on a farm in the village.

Although she had so little money to spend, shopping took up a considerable amount of her time. The village was too small to have a shop of its own, though one of the old women always had a few sweets displayed in her cottage window, and another woman brought back a few faggots and pieces of black pudding from the market town to sell at a small profit. Twice a week, Mrs Strudwick walked the three miles into town and back again, often in company with other women from the village. She brought back bread and meat and other necessities. Since the railway station had opened in the town, a number of new shops had been opened, selling many different kinds of goods, which were too expensive for her to buy. There seemed to be more strangers there, too.

A number of pedlars or packmen visited the village regularly. Some of them came on foot, carrying their goods in wicker baskets suspended from a wooden yoke on their shoulders; others came on a horse with wicker panniers strapped on either side; a few with a horse and cart. The pot-and-pan man, who also sold sand for the floor, was a regular caller, and so was the rag-and-bone man, who gave her children a windmill on a stick if she had anything to spare for him. There were also a couple of packmen who came out from the town with draperies and clothes that you could buy by weekly instalments.

They had all been coming to the village for many years and she usually had a chat with them at the back door even if she wasn't going to buy anything, as it provided a break in the daily routine. Then there were the gipsy women, with their brown, wrinkled faces, large gold earrings, and red handkerchiefs around their heads, who came in the summer with clothes pegs and wooden spoons, while their husbands were working in the hayfields. From time to time the old knifegrinder and the chairmender visited the village, too. Until quite recently there had been another regular weekly visitor—the coalman who came round on Saturday. She'd always bought four stone of coal for 1s. Coal had been a luxury then, but since the railway had been opened in the

Children had to make their own amusements at that time

market town it had become much cheaper. Mr Bennett brought it in his wagons from the station twice a year and delivered it at cost price to his workers.

But that afternoon there was an unexpected visitor to her cottage. She was just getting ready to go out when she heard the sound of the postman's horn. A few seconds later, a horse, snorting and neighing, stopped outside her cottage. As the postman called out her name, she went outside and took the letter from him. It was the first time the postman had ever called at her home, though she had seen him delivering letters to the vicarage and the big house

Straw 'dollies' in the shape of a bird were often attached to the thatch covering of a haystack or a house; and (right) an iron cauldron in which food was cooked on the open fire

on the other side of the village many times. She knew from the writing on the envelope that it was from her eldest daughter, Ann. After looking at the envelope, back and front, and showing it to Sarah, she propped it up on the mantelpiece, where it would remain until her husband came home.

Mrs Strudwick closed the front door. Then, telling Sarah to be good, she went out and locked the back door behind her, putting the big iron key in the wicker basket she was carrying on her arm. She walked along the narrow lane towards the village, between high banks which were spattered here and there with little green and yellow clumps of primroses. She passed Mrs Stevens's cottage, where she had been to buy the loaf of bread that morning. A little farther on, there was a slightly larger cottage, with a small adjacent yard stacked with timber which was weathering in the open air, and a small shed where Mr Gregory, the wheelwright, worked. Farther on again, there was a small cottage, the home of Polly Cook who worked with Mrs Strudwick's husband on Mr Bennett's farm. She walked across the village green where a couple of geese owned by the innkeeper were grazing. On the far side of the green she could see Mary Sutton, a little, twisted cripple, dressed in black, limping towards her cottage in the woods. She lived in isolation in a small single-roomed hut, with a torn thatched roof which gave only partial protection from the wind and the rain. All the villagers avoided her; she was reputed to have the 'evil eye'. Everyone believed that she had obtained her powers of witchcraft from her old mother, who had been found by the vicar's wife one winter's day huddled up dead in her rag bed on the earthen floor of her hut, with no sign of a fire in the hearth, and the inside walls frozen over by a solid sheet of ice. Her black cat was crouched by her side. Mary Sutton was often blamed for many of the disasters in the village—the sudden death of a pig, an epidemic of measles.

The village was Mrs Strudwick's whole world. She had never seen the sea; she had never visited London, or, indeed, any other large town. The only time she had been farther than the market town was in her childhood. Every Christmas she used to walk with her family to see her uncle who lived in a village six miles away. She knew everyone in her village, their jobs and their characters, when they had married, when their children had been born, when their own parents had died. Some of the families had lived in the village for generations; their ancestors lay buried in the churchyard beneath a simple mound of earth, unmarked by any headstone, though one or two of the craftsmen's graves had wooden headboards. Because so many families had lived in the village for generations, many people were related by marriage. Between two of the family groups in the village, there was bitter rivalry caused by some remote feud, of whose origin even the members of the families now retained only a confused memory.

It was towards the churchyard that Mrs Strudwick turned. Just before she reached it, she went into the vicarage and followed the path which led round to the back of the house. She went into an old, large barn, with a long wooden table at one end. Before she had been there very long, one or two other women from the village also arrived, including Sally Ford, who had a bruised eye. Although they said nothing, Mrs Strudwick and all the other women knew what had happened: Sally's husband, John Ford, had been drinking too much again.

They all waited in a corner of the barn, talking slowly to each other and glancing furtively at the door from time to time. After several minutes, the vicar's wife entered, followed by two of her daughters, laughing and chattering to each other. They were carrying a number of parcels which they placed on the table. The women from the village moved a little closer. As the vicar's wife called out their names, they stepped forward and were given their parcel, which they then untied. Each parcel contained the clothes they had ordered through the village clothing club. Every week they paid a few pence to the churchwarden and every year the squire's wife added a pound or two to the total sum which had been collected.

The gipsy 'queen'

Packmen, selling goods of various kinds, were regular callers at the villages. This photograph was taken at Willersey, near Broadway, Worcestershire, towards the end of the nineteenth century

The women ordered their clothes from a tradesman in the market town, but the parcels were not sent direct to them, but to the vicar's wife, so that she could make sure that the women had ordered only warm, sensible clothes and nothing that was unsuitable for their station in life. The village women, however, found it fairly easy to get round this. In the following week the draper's pedlar always did a brisk trade selling fringes, coloured ribbons, and ornamental buttons, which the women then sewed on their plain new clothes.

The vicar's wife was also in charge of another charity which gave bread and blankets to the 'deserving poor' just before Christmas. Another charity in the village also gave a coat and 10s to any man who had worked for thirty years without claiming poor law relief—and a certificate. Apart from these charities, each family had to depend entirely on their own efforts and to live on the small wages they could earn, unless they wanted to apply for official parish relief to the Board of Guardians. But Mrs Strudwick, and all the other women, knew that all you'd ever get from them was a stony stare and a couple of shillings a week if your children were almost dying. They'd just as soon put you in the workhouse as look at you.

After Mrs Strudwick had collected her parcel, she put it in her wicker basket and set out for home. On the way back she was thinking about the fringe she'd sew on Naomi's new Sunday dress.

6. EVENING

By 4.30 p.m. Mrs Strudwick was at home again. Naomi and David arrived back from school about a quarter of an hour later. They stared wide-eyed when Mrs Strudwick showed them the letter from their sister, Ann, and were delighted when they saw the new clothes. Mrs Strudwick gave all her children a slice of bread and treacle and then built up the fire with some small pieces of coal. She put the cauldron containing their dinner on the hook of the hanger above the fire. Once it was boiling, she raised it up a little by means of the ratchet until it was just simmering, and gave the stew a turn or two with a wooden spoon. Later on, after John had returned from his day's work on the farm, she made a few dumplings and dropped them from the wooden spoon into the stew.

Her husband returned home just before 6.45 and she immediately gave him the letter from their daughter. He looked at it carefully, tore the envelope open, and then gave the letter back to her to read. Apart from Sunday school, he had never been to school, and all he could remember from the education he had received at his Sunday school were some passages from the Bible, a few of which he could still repeat by heart. Mrs Strudwick, however, had been to the National school and to Sunday school as well. With Naomi by her side she sat down at the table and slowly puzzled out the words. Neither she nor her daughter could fully understand every word, but they were able to get the gist of the letter. Ann was well, had good food to eat, and though she didn't like her mistress much, her master was kind to her and had said that she could have three days' holiday in the summer, so she was coming home.

They were all delighted with the news. They hadn't seen Ann or heard anything of her ever since she'd gone off by train some months ago with her few personal possessions wrapped up in two large handkerchiefs. Among them was her most prized possession, a canvas sampler she had embroidered with a decorative border of birds and flowers and the following verse:

> Ann Strudwick is my name
> England is my nation
> Marley is my dwelling place
> And Christ is my Salvation.

It was through her skill in needlework that she had obtained the job in London.

Some of the local pottery was crudely made, like this washing bowl with a little recess in the lip to hold the soap

A rushlight holder

Young girls practised their needlework by embroidering samplers. Some of them included their name, age and place of birth

57

Skittles was one of the favourite games in village inns

The rector's wife had encouraged her by giving her extra sewing from her own household to do, and had also supplied the piece of canvas for the sampler. Finally, she had recommended her to a friend of hers in London who was in need of a domestic servant. Ann earned £15 a year—almost half her father's wages—and had much better food to eat, too. Mrs Strudwick was very pleased that Ann had done so well; when she came to stay, she'd have to make up a bed for her on the kitchen floor.

After they'd all heard what was in the letter, Mr Strudwick went into the back kitchen to wash and shave. Normally, he shaved only twice a week, on Wednesdays and Saturdays, but he always had a shave if he was going out in the evening. He washed his face and hands in a rough earthenware bowl, with a little cup on the rim to contain the soap, and then shaved his upper lip and chin carefully with his open 'cut-throat' razor, leaving the fringe of whiskers around his face untouched. He examined himself in a piece of cracked looking-glass and combed his hair. Meanwhile Mrs Strudwick had been getting the children clean for dinner and Naomi had been laying the table.

By now it was becoming dark but Mrs Strudwick still did not light a candle, as they were too expensive to waste. She dished up the dinner, serving her husband first and giving him the major share as she always did—two dumplings, potatoes, and plenty of strong, coarse cabbage all boiled up in the remainder of the previous day's stew. The oldest boy, John, was served next.

58

She went on through the rest of her family, so that by the time she came to her baby boy and herself there was very little left, but for the greasy liquid, which they'd mop up with a piece of bread. Hunks of bread and mugs of weak tea were the only accompaniment to the stew.

The meal was soon finished. Mr Strudwick went into the back kitchen, took off his boots and inspected them in the fading light. One or two nails were missing from the soles, so he took out a hammer and his cobbler's last and knocked in a few nails. Every week he inspected the boots of his whole family and did what he could to keep them in good repair as they were so expensive to replace. He had to take them to the cobbler for major repairs.

After he had said goodbye, he picked up two shillings that he had left in a pot on a shelf in the back kitchen and walked off in the dusk towards the village. Although it was only just after 7.30, the village was almost deserted. A few of the cottages were already in total darkness; most old people went to bed at dusk or even earlier. Some of the other cottages were illuminated only by the small, flickering flames of a fire in the open hearth. Here and there, a solitary candle was burning, and in a few homes he could see the feeble, spluttering glow of a rushlight. It was a messy form of lighting, which needed great attention, as the rushlight had to be pulled up an inch or so at a time from its holder and each one burnt for only about half an hour. But some of the older and poorer people in the village still relied on rushlights, gathering the rushes in summer, stripping off the tough green outer peel, drying the stem and finally drawing it through a pan of melted mutton or bacon fat.

Apart from the voices of a group of children still playing outside the back door of one of the cottages and the croaking of frogs from a nearby pond, there was a deep, undisturbed silence everywhere. Samuel walked on over the village green, where in the summer evenings some of the local farmers' sons practised cricket, towards the welcoming windows of the village inn. The inn, with its china-bowled paraffin lamps, its wood fire, its heavy, high-backed settle, its benches, its warmth, its friendship, its games, its songs was the only place of entertainment in the village. You could learn what was going on in the rest of the country by reading the newspapers, which were provided free, or by listening to the other men reading them, if you couldn't read yourself. Up to last year, you could always have a game of dominoes or a game of skittles in the adjoining skittle alley, with its benches and its neatly clipped yew hedges, for a quart of beer; but the government had now stopped such forms of gambling. At the same time, all country inns had been ordered to close by ten at night, though they could still open at six in the morning. There always seemed to be so many changes now, that Samuel sometimes wondered what would happen next.

He did not go to the inn every night, as he could not afford it, but he always tried to go there some time on Saturday night. This was the most popular

Village friendly societies had elaborately decorated banners. This one comes from North Curry, Somerset

night. They usually had a visit from a gipsy with his fiddle or a ballad singer, who sold printed copies of his songs and of stories of executions and murders for $\frac{1}{2}$d. Friday night was one of the quieter nights. Samuel walked into the inn and greeted the innkeeper and the other men and walked past them into an inner room. A number of other men were already gathered around a table. A large, silk-embroidered banner was hanging from the wall and a long staff with a brass emblem at the top was propped up against the wall beside it.

Every month the village benefit society held its meeting in this room. Each member paid 1s a month and if he was sick and unable to work he received 1s a day for six weeks and 6d a day for six weeks after that. Although Samuel had been a member for more than twenty years, he'd never had to ask for any benefit yet. He wondered sometimes if he'd ever be able to get any help if he needed it, as the funds were running so low. The trouble was that as the older members died off, the younger men weren't coming in to replace them. Instead, they were joining another friendly society, the Ancient Order of Foresters, which had branches all over the country. But Samuel remained faithful to the village club, because he'd paid in so much money, because the

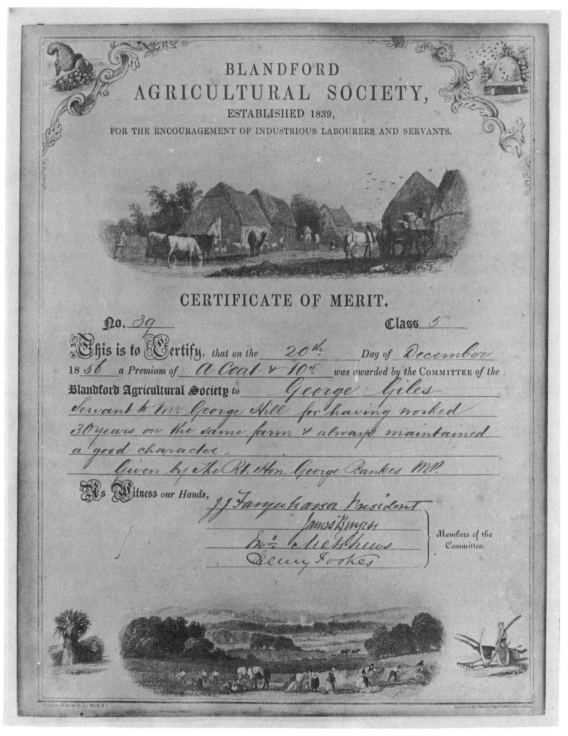

BLANDFORD
AGRICULTURAL SOCIETY,
ESTABLISHED 1839,
FOR THE ENCOURAGEMENT OF INDUSTRIOUS LABOURERS AND SERVANTS.

CERTIFICATE OF MERIT.

No. *39*   Class *5*

This is to Certify, that on the *20th* Day of *December*
18*56* a Premium of *A Coat & 10s* was awarded by the COMMITTEE of the
Blandford Agricultural Society to *George Giles*
Servant to Mr George Hill for having worked
30 years on the same farm & always maintained
a good character
Given by the Rt. Hon. George Bankes M.P.

As Witness our Hands, *J J Farquharson President*
James Bryer
Wm Matthews   Members of the
Henry Fookes   Committee.

There were many local charities for the 'deserving poor' which,
however, were not particularly generous

61

members were all his friends, and because it still provided one of the most entertaining days of the whole year.

Every year they had their annual dinner which was paid for partly out of club funds. Early in the morning the members would all form up outside the inn and, headed by a three-piece band and two men carrying their banner, they would march around the district, asking the squire, the vicar, and the farmers for a subscription to their dinner, which they held later that night in the village inn. In the afternoon there was always a small fair on the village green with a few gipsies selling gingerbread, toys and nuts; another gipsy playing a fiddle; and an Aunt Sally stall, where you threw sticks at a clay pipe in the mouth of a wooden effigy of an old woman.

It was one of the highlights of their year, which was anticipated and then remembered for many days, in the same way as Christmas Day, the harvest supper, and the annual fairs in the market town. There were two fairs in the town in the autumn. One was devoted in the morning to the serious business of selling horses, cattle and sheep, and in the afternoon and evening to entertainment. Whole families walked in from miles around and saved for weeks so that they could buy gingerbread and nuts for their children and themselves; try their luck on the shooting range; see a two-headed monster or the performing fleas; send their children on the roundabout pulled by a horse.

A month later a hiring fair was held in the same town. There was the same blowing of horns and beating of drums outside the gaily decorated stalls in the streets, but it was attended by fewer children. Its main purpose was for farmers to hire for the coming year cowmen, shepherds, ploughmen and the young lads to help them, who lived at the farm and were paid 4s or so a week. The men all wore some sign of their calling in their hats: the ploughman had a twist of whipcord; the cowman a wisp of cow hair; the shepherd a piece of wool. When the farmer had hired a man, he would seal the bargain with a shilling. Most of the men went off to the nearest public house, where they spent the afternoon and evening drinking and chatting to the local girls and domestic servants who always seemed to be present on these occasions.

Apart from these annual events, there were few other arranged entertainments in their lives—only an occasional talk by a missionary about his work in far-off lands, or a penny reading, where you paid 1d to hear extracts from the classics being read. And the monthly meeting of the benefit club. Samuel paid his monthly subscription, bought a pint of beer for twopence and an

Broadsheets about murders were popular reading, and executions attracted large crowds of spectators. Public executions were stopped a few years after the date of the execution described on the opposite page

CONFESSION & EXECUTION

OF

NOAH AUSTIN,

FOR THE MURDER OF

JAMES ALLEN, of Upper Heyford.

On Wednesday, the 11th inst., the unhappy man was visited by his two sisters, and Miss Allen, the daughter of the murdered man, to whom he had paid his addresses; the interview was a very painful one, but he assured them that he was perfectly innocent. On Wednesday last, the final interview between the father and son took place; on the morning of that day, Mr. Austin, accompanied by an unmarried daughter, visited Noah Austin, in the presence of the officials of the gaol. Mr. Austin, who is well known and respected as a local preacher in connexion with the Wesleyan denomination, entreated his son to relieve his conscience by making a confession of the crime, inasmuch as there was not the slightest hope of his sentence being interfered with by an exercise of the Royal clemency. The conduct of the prisoner in the first instance was of a very violent character. He upbraided his father in almost menacing language for wishing him to confess to the perpetration of a crime of which he protested his innocence. Ultimately, however, the wretched man made a statement to the Chaplain, the Rev. J. Thorp, which was taken down in writing, and subsequently attested in the presence of Dr. Wynter, the President of St. John's College, one of the county magistrates, and Mr. J. M. Davenport, the Clerk of the Peace.

THE CONFESSION

" In the Condemned Cell, Oxford Castle, this 18th of March, 1863, in the presence of the Rev. Philip Wynter, D.D., a Justice of the Peace of the County of Oxford, the prisoner, Noah Austin, being asked if he wished to make any statement, voluntarily said as follows:—

" I did not buy the pistol with the intention of shooting Mr. Allen. On Wednesday, the 11th of February, Mr. Allen had behaved ill to his daughter by turning her out of doors. She sent for me on the following morning, and, after telling me of his treatment, said she 'wished some accident would happen to him.' I said, 'I'll see, but we shall be found out.' She said, 'O, no we shan't.' She said, 'be sure you come down in the evening, and we'll arrange it;' and my impression was that she wished her father to be got rid of. I went to the Mill again on Thursday evening, and saw Miss Allen. She again said she 'wished that something would happen to her father.' More words passed between us, but I do not remember exactly what. The father then came in tipsy, and I left to avoid a quarrel between us, as, when he was in that state he could not say anything against me bad enough. I felt sure that Miss Allen wished me to get rid of her father; and I left the Mill with the intention of carrying out what I believed to be her wish, but I do not think she knew that I should do so the next day, though I am sure she thought I should do so at some time. I then determined to go to Bicester the next day with my father for that purpose. I carried the pistol in my pocket.

I could not have done it unless I had had some drink. I went to a strange house in Bicester that I might not be known (either the Nag's Head or King's Head), and had about two glasses of strong beer. I then returned with Mr. Allen, as stated in the evidence; and when sitting by his side, raised the pistol to his cheek, and fired the first shot, which caused him at once to fall over the off side of the cart; and whilst falling, I fired the other shot; and when he was lying on the ground, I took the purse out of his pocket. There were only a few shillings in it. I knew he had the £5 note in his breast pocket and the cheque; but I did not want his money, but took the purse to make it believe that he had been robbed as well as murdered. I fastened the horse to the gate, and then ran towards Upper Heyford, as stated in the evidence. On my way to the Mill, I placed the pistol in the gig, in my father's rick-yard; I then went to the Mill, and afterwards returned home, and went up to my sister's bed-room, and put the purse and the key in my desk, as found by the police.

I make this statement because I wish to ease the mind of my poor afflicted father, to whom I have occasioned so much sorrow, and because I am sure that I cannot be forgiven by God, while I refuse to confess the wrongs I have committed against man."

" This statement was voluntarily made before me this 18th of March, 1863—P. WYNTER, a Justice of the Peace, in the County of Oxford, and a Visiting Justice of the Oxford Castle.

(Signed)   NOAH AUSTIN.

THE EXECUTION

(By Electric Telegraph)

NOAH AUSTIN was executed this morning (Tuesday, March 24th, 1863), at 8 o'clock, on the tower of Oxford Castle, for the murder of JAMES ALLEN. Never on any similar occasion (excepting perhaps the execution of Kalabergo, on Monday, March 22nd, 1852) had a greater number of people congregated together. Long before the time fixed for the execution of the wretched man, every space which afforded an opportunity of witnessing the awful spectacle was completely filled; and the streets leading to the scene were almost impassable. Every precaution was adopted by the authorities to prevent any ill consequences resulting from the pressure of the crowd, as an immense number of persons was naturally anticipated.

A little before 8 o'clock, the solemn bell of the chapel tolled at intervals, and at 8 o'clock the mournful procession proceeded from the ante-chapel. When on the drop the wretched criminal changed his countenance, and looked extremely pale, the white cap was soon drawn over his face, and in a few seconds he paid the penalty of his dreadful crime. Calcraft was the public executioner.

J. A. TAPLIN, Printer, 36, Parson's St, Banbury

63

ounce of tobacco for the same amount, and settled back in his chair to enjoy himself.

Meanwhile, back at home, Mrs Strudwick had washed up and put the children to bed. She sat huddled round the dying embers of the fire, finishing the last gloves by the spluttering light of a stump of candle. Sometimes, at night when she wasn't working, she'd sit in the firelight, going to bed when the last glowing embers of the fire had faded into the dark. By nine o'clock she had finished the last glove. She snuffed out the candle and went up to bed in the dark.

She soon fell asleep. Some time later she was awakened by the sound of her husband clattering up the stairs. He staggered as he came into the room and knocked against a chair. She hissed to him to be quiet. She heard him undressing. He got into bed and settled down to try to get warm. Soon all she could hear was her husband's heavy breathing in the dark.

Suddenly, from the direction of the village, there was a great din of kettles and pans being banged with sticks, and much shouting. Naomi woke up, frightened, but Mrs Strudwick told her to go to sleep again. There was nothing to be afraid of. Mrs Strudwick knew what was happening. Some of the men in the village were giving John Ford the 'rough music' for giving his wife a black eye again. It served him right. Mrs Strudwick smiled to herself, turned over, and settled down to sleep. Another day had passed.

7. THE NATIONAL SCENE

In the 1870s the Strudwicks' way of life was being repeated in thousands of cottages, on hundreds of farms, and in dozens of schools in many parts of the country. Every incident in the narrative is authentic and must have happened many hundreds of thousands of times, though not necessarily all in the course of one day. Indeed, in some ways the Strudwicks' day was more crowded with events than most would have been. One incident alone, the receipt of the letter from their daughter working in London, would have been sufficient to mark the day off as exceptional.

Nevertheless, the Strudwicks can stand as true representatives of the farm workers and their families living at that time. Naturally, each family lived to a certain extent in its own way. Even within the limits of their restricted budgets, there was a little room for individual manoeuvre. Some men drank much more than Samuel Strudwick did; a few—members of a strict religious sect—did not drink at all. Men like Willy East, who had the opportunity to keep a pig and the capital to buy one, or a farmer who would subsidise them, were better off. Usually, they sold most of it to a butcher, and kept only a few small joints for themselves. Those men who were willing to take the risks could increase their income by snaring rabbits or game and selling them to the publican or game-dealer. Penalties for poaching, however, were severe: the maximum punishment for taking game or rabbits at night was imprisonment with hard labour for up to three months for the first offence, and up to six months for subsequent offences. If three or more men were caught poaching together at night, armed with guns or other offensive weapons, they could be sentenced to penal servitude for three to fourteen years.

The farm worker was also greatly affected by the attitude of his employer. Some of the large landowners, whose farms were run by bailiffs or farm stewards, could afford to be charitable to their workers; but many of the smaller farmers were themselves hard pressed. The average-sized farm of a hundred acres in the south was run by a working farmer, who employed five or six farm labourers. In the north and west, the average-sized farm was smaller, about seventy acres, and with just two or three labourers.[1] Some of these farmers were much worse to their employees than Mr Bennett was, but

[1] Cf. T. W. Fletcher, 'The Great Depression of English Agriculture, 1873–1896', in W. E. Minchinton (ed.), *Essays in Agrarian History*, David and Charles, 1968, vol. 2, p. 247.

it is somewhat doubtful if there were many who were much better or more considerate.

There were also considerable regional variations in the way farm workers lived a century ago. Differences between counties were much greater than they are now. Farm wagons, for example, were usually painted in different colours in each county, so that they were as distinguishable as modern makes of motor-cars. The ploughman's command to his horses to turn left ranged from 'half-back' in Yorkshire to something like 'woi' in Kent. Dialects were so distinctive that a farm worker from one county would have had great difficulty in understanding a farm labourer from another. A man from one of the farming villages around Sheffield would have spoken in the following way: 'Hah, they'n better toimes on't nah, booath e heitin and clooas; we'n had menni a mess a nettle porridge an brawis on a Sunda mo'nin, for us brekfast.'[1] (Huh! They have better times of it now, both in eating and clothes; we've had many a dish of nettle broth and porridge on a Sunday morning for our breakfast.) The man from Sussex would have talked in a different way: 'There warn't any grass at all when we fust come here; naun but a passel o' gurt old tots and tussicks.'[2] (There wasn't any grass at all when we first came here; nothing but a parcel of great old weeds and coarse grass.'

In the same way working and living conditions varied greatly from one region of the country to another. In Scotland, farm cottages were very scarce and many of them had no more than one room. A large number of farm servants, as they were called, lived in bothies, long huts where they lived and slept together and sometimes cooked their own meals. But there was far more concern about providing a good education for their children than there was in other parts of Britain. On the isolated sheep farms, five or six shepherds clubbed together to employ a tutor for their children.[3]

Wales presented a different picture. Schooling was worse, partly because of the language difficulty. Dairy work and milking was often done by young women who were employed as farm servants from the age of eleven or twelve. Apart from that, many of the small farms devoted to darying and rearing cattle, employed only family help.[4]

---

[1] A. Bywater, *Sheffield Dialect*, Wakefield, 3rd edn, 1877, p. 32.
[2] Rev. W. D. Parish, *A Dictionary of the Sussex Dialect and Collection of Provincialisms in Use in the County of Sussex*, Lewes, 1875, p. 123.
[3] Cf. *Fourth Report of Commissioners, Royal Commission on the Employment of Children, Young Persons, and Women in Agriculture*, Parliamentary Papers, House of Commons, vol. XIII, 1870, pp. 5–26, London, 1870.
[4] Cf. ibid., *Third Report*, pp. 5–19.

Some of the biggest contrasts were presented by the north, and the west and south of England. In some parts of the north, farmers let a couple of acres of land to their employees so that they could keep cows. Wages in Morpeth, Northumberland, were on average 20s a week, while in Sedgefield, Durham, they were 24s. In Cerne, Dorset, on the other hand, they were only 9s a week.[1] Farm workers in Devonshire were among the worst off in the whole country. Wages were usually 7s a week and rarely more than 8s, plus a free daily quart of cider, which was so undrinkable that the farmer couldn't sell it.[2]

The real differences might not have been so high as these figures suggest, as some wages were still paid in kind—free beer, cider, potatoes—and on many farms there were opportunities for paid overtime, such as weeding and hoeing, in addition to the bonus payment for the harvest. Nevertheless, the farm worker in the north was usually much better off than his brother in the south, mainly because higher wages in the industrial towns forced farmers to compete for labour. The highest-paid workers in all parts of the country were the men in charge of animals, who always worked a seven-day week. Some Scottish shepherds received £60 a year and a number of perquisites.

The similarities in the farm workers' way of life, however, were much greater than the individual and regional differences. In whatever part of the country he lived, the farm labourer led an exhausting, frugal and restricted life. One way of seeing this more clearly is to contrast the position of the farm worker, with his low wages and scanty possessions, with that of just one of the landed aristocracy of the time, as described in one contemporary account:

The landed possessions of the Duke of Sutherland are as follows:–

Sutherland	. . . .	1,176,454 acres
Shropshire	. . . .	17,495 ,,
Staffordshire	. . . .	12,744 ,,
Yorkshire	. . . .	1,853 ,,

The Duchess also owns a small estate, consisting of 149,879 acres, in Ross. We have thus a grand total of one million, three hundred and fifty-eight thousand, four hundred and twenty-five acres, producing a gross annual rental of £140,928. The Duke is also owner of the following seats:– Dunrobin Castle, Loch Inver House, House of Tongue, Tarbet House, Castle Leod, all in Scotland; and Stafford House, St James's Park; Trentham Hall, in Staffordshire; Lilleshall Hall, in Shropshire; and Cliefden, in Bucks . . .

[1] Cf. *Returns of Agricultural Labourers' Average Weekly Earnings*, Parliamentary Papers, House of Commons, vol. LIII, 1873, London, 1873.
[2] Cf. Francis George Heath, *The English Peasantry*, Frederick Warne, 1874, pp. 138–58.

The 1,176,454 acres in Sutherland have been almost entirely acquired by legal robbery, and taken possession of by high-handed cruelty. The Sutherland estate is the largest case of this kind, though in some respects by no means the worst, since several great landowners in the Highlands have depopulated the country to make deer forests, while the Sutherland-Leveson-Gowers depopulated it to form sheep farms . . .

It was determined to convert the country into sheep farms, and to attain that object the population were to be driven to the seacoast to subsist by fishing . . . In March, 1814, the people of two large parishes were summoned to quit in May. Before the day of eviction came the heather was set on fire; many of their cattle were thus starved, and the rest had to be sold at great disadvantage. While many of the men were away selling their cattle, the houses were pulled down over the people's heads, and then set on fire . . . An eye-witness of the scene says:—'I ascended a height at about eleven o'clock in the evening, and counted 250 blazing houses.'[1]

The truly dismal quality of the farm workers' life a century ago has been obscured by the pretty patina formed over reality with the passing of the years. A long line of writers has retailed a picture of idyllic rural bliss. Among them was the minor poet, Felicia Hemans, who wrote in *The Houses of England*:

> . . . The cottage homes of England!
> By thousands on her plains,
> They are smiling o'er the silvery brooks,
> And round the hamlet fanes.
> Through glowing orchards forth they peep,
> Each from its nook of leaves;
> And fearless there the lowly sleep,
> As the bird beneath their eaves.
>
> The free, fair homes of England!
> Long, long, in hut and hall,
> May hearts of native proof be rear'd
> To guard each hallow'd wall!
> And green for ever be the groves,
> And bright the flowery sod,
> Where first the child's glad spirit loves
> Its country and its God![2]

---

[1] Noblesse Oblige (i.e. Howard Evans), *Our Old Nobility*, London, 1879, pp. 33–5.
[2] *The Poems of Felicia Hemans*, William Blackwood and Sons, Edinburgh and London, new edn, 1849, p. 412.

Some farm workers lived in cottages of this kind. This photograph was taken a few years ago near Holsworthy, Devon

It is still possible to read in a few books published even now of the farm worker of the 1870s returning home from a long and hard, but healthy, day's work in the fields to his picturesquely furnished cottage with its blazing log fire. In fact, few farm workers had a chance to burn logs, as many farmers would not let them pick up dead branches from their fields even after a storm. Their cottages were anything but picturesquely, or even adequately, furnished. Most farm labourers had very few possessions. The one or two luxuries they did possess, like the Strudwicks' pair of bellows and their broken Toby jug, had usually been given to them by a farmer or purchased cheaply at a farm sale. It is ironic that there are probably more fakes of the one object they did possess in some abundance—ornamental horse brasses—than there are of almost any other relic. These brasses were awarded as prizes to ploughmen in the ploughing matches organised by agricultural societies, and were among their most treasured possessions.

Husbands and wives often worked together in the harvest. This photograph taken at Brimpton, Berkshire, in 1895, shows Martha and Francis Dyer, with the scythesman in the middle

Smocks were still worn by a few old farm workers at the beginning of the present century. Notice how his trousers are tied up just below the knees

But those relics of a vanished age, copper warming pans, pewter salt cellars and pepper pots, roasting spits, and bronze trivets—the 'Victoriana' which is now so popular among some antique dealers—were to be found only rarely in cottages in the 1870s. They came mostly from the homes of squires, farmers and the middle class. The illustrations of relics in this book are far more representative of what farm workers possessed.

In the same way we can still sometimes read of farm labourers eating good plain meals of meat, home-baked bread and fruit from their own gardens. Reality again was different. Most of the meat they bought was fat and of the poorest quality; even those who kept a pig had to sell most of it to pay for their rent or clothes. Similarly, many were forced to sell the apples from the trees in their own gardens to pay their yearly bills. Home baking of bread was impossible for the many wives who had no ovens. They had to buy their bread, much of which was adulterated with alum, from bakers in the towns. A survey carried out by the medical journal, the *Lancet*, in 1872, showed that half of the samples of bread examined were adulterated; there was a great improvement following the passing of the Sale of Food and Drugs Act in 1875, under which heavy fines could be imposed for adulterating food.[1]

The picture of the happy, conservative, servile peasant is one of the great historical distortions. Even the Hammonds, great historians of the farm workers' struggles, called the rising of 1830 'the last labourers' revolt', as if there had been no strikes in 1872 and as if Joseph Arch, who organized them, had never existed.[2] From what evidence there is, it seems likely that just beneath the apparently placid surface of the countryside, there was seething discontent, which erupted in the riots of the 1830s, simmered for another forty years, and broke out again in the 1870s.

In 1830 there were riots all over southern England, East Anglia and parts of the Midlands, led, so it was said, by a mysterious character called Captain Swing. Threshing machines were destroyed; corn ricks burned; and higher wages personally demanded from farmers by deputations of workers. The riots were followed by savage punishments. Nineteen men and boys were executed, all but three for arson; 481 transported to Australia and Tasmania; and another 644 imprisoned.[3] For many years afterwards the shadow of the revolt still hung heavily over many villages; the missing fathers and sons bore

---

[1] Cf. John Burnett, *Plenty and Want: A Social History of Diet in England from 1815 to the Present Day*, Penguin Books, 1968, p. 263.
[2] Despite this, J. L. and Barbara Hammonds' *The Village Labourer*, first published in 1911, remains the most readable survey of farm workers' conditions in the late eighteenth and early nineteenth centuries, even though some of their findings have now been superseded.
[3] Cf. E. J. Hobsbawm and George Rudé, *Captain Swing*, Lawrence and Wishart, 1969, pp. 262–3.

a silent testimony to the savage reprisals that had been taken against them then. The 'Swing' riots were the farm workers' equivalent of the urban workers' Peterloo.

Another twist of the repressive screw was applied in Dorset in 1834 when the brothers, George and James Loveless, James Hammett, James Brine, and Thomas Stanfield and his son John—the 'Tolpuddle Martyrs'—were sentenced to transportation for seven years for administering illegal oaths to members of a trade union. Owing to the pressure of public opinion, the rest of their sentences was remitted in 1836.

For the next thirty years there were a few isolated strikes and sporadic attempts to form unions in the countryside, which had little success until the end of the 1860s when some unions and associations were formed on a county basis. It was some measure of the continuing discontent that Joseph Arch should have had such a phenomenal and immediate success with his creation of a National Agricultural Labourers' Union in 1872. It was founded in May and a year later it had over 70,000 members. Farm workers went on strike in support of their demands for higher wages; but in 1873–4 farmers retaliated by locking out the strikers and evicting some of them from their cottages. By the summer of 1874 the union had capitulated and the men resumed work. The revolt, however, did succeed in putting up wages by 1s to 3s a week in some places. After the return to work, some men broke away from the national movement to form their own local unions, and support gradually dwindled until by 1889 there were fewer than 5,000 members.[1] It was not until 1906 that George (later Sir George) Edwards succeeded in setting up a successful union in the eastern counties, which became a national union in 1910 and adopted its present name of the National Union of Agricultural and Allied Workers in 1968.[2]

The capitulation by Arch's union coincided with the start of an agricultural depression which lasted from about 1875 to 1895. Not all farmers were equally affected, in fact livestock and dairy farmers prospered. But a succession of extremely wet years brought disaster to many arable farmers, whose wheat lay blackened in the fields. Many of them went bankrupt. At that time, too, cheap wheat started to flow in from the vast prairies of the New World. All of these changes meant fewer jobs for both casual and permanent workers, and accelerated the drift away from the land which had already started in the 1860s.

In 1851 about one-quarter of all employed men in Britain worked on farms;

[1] Cf. Christabel S. Orwin and Edith H. Whetham, *History of British Agriculture, 1846–1914*, Longmans Green, 1964, pp. 228–39; and Reg Groves, *Sharpen the Sickle*, Porcupine Press, London, 1949, pp. 39–80.
[2] For details of the formation see George Edwards, *From Crow Scaring to Westminster*, Labour Publishing Co., London, 1922.

by 1901, the number had been reduced by about half—to 12 per cent. Many farm workers left Britain for good, finding a new and better life in Canada, Australia or New Zealand. In Canada, agricultural workers from Britain were in great demand and it was reported that in some places they could earn as much as 16s or 18s a *day* during the harvest season. Such high rates of pay were exceptional, but wages were on average much higher than they were in Britain and some prices were lower, with beef and mutton costing 3d a lb. and pork 4d. Not all the emigrants were satisfied with their new life, but thousands wrote enthusiastic letters to their relatives in Britain. As news of these great opportunities, described in such letters as the following, circulated in the villages, more and more young men were encouraged to emigrate:

4 October 1868

. . . Montreal is a fine large city, and I remained in Montreal for three weeks waiting to see a gentleman farmer, and seeing him he engaged with me for 12 months, and longer if I suit him; and I have been at my place for three weeks, and I like the place very well, and I have to help milk, and this winter time I shall have the cattle to see to. And I have a home, and a good great garden, and all my firewood, and £50 a year, and the boy is getting 16s 8d a month this winter, and in the summer he will have 25s a month. So the Lord has made my way very clear indeed for me, and I have much to praise the Lord for. Where I am now is about 120 miles from Montreal, and one of the finest places in Canada. We are all comfortable and happy, and the wife sends her kindest and best love to you all.[1]

Thousands more young people who were unable or unwilling to try their luck abroad, migrated to the towns, attracted by higher wages and a shorter working week. Some worked in factories; some joined the police; some became grooms. The railway network, which covered most of the country by the 1870s, helped to break down the isolation of the villages by making travel to distant towns much easier, and also provided an alternative source of rural employment for the discontented sons of farm labourers. Towards the end of the nineteenth century, the development of the modern bicycle made it possible for some of the better-educated sons to take up employment in towns near their homes as shop assistants or clerks.

Improvements in the national system of education decreased illiteracy in the country and eventually helped to broaden the outlook of young children. In the early part of the nineteenth century education in villages had been

[1] W. Frank Lynn, *Pamphlet for Working Men on Emigration, Labour, Wages, and Free Grants of Land*, Canadian News Office, London, 1869, p. 7.

During the second half of the nineteenth century, branches of the national friendly society—the Ancient Order of Foresters—were set up in many villages. The club day remained one of the main events of the year. This photograph was taken at Iffley, Oxfordshire, about 1900

provided at dame's schools, which were sometimes run by the local curate, and at Sunday schools. From about 1840 onwards an increasing number of village schools were built by the two national societies: The National Society for Promoting the Education of the Poor in the Principles of the Established Church, and the British and Foreign School Society. Although a few parents kept their children at school until the age of twelve or thirteen, many boys left at nine or ten to start regular employment on a farm. In some villages, the vicar opened night schools to help these early-leavers. But most villagers received a scanty education and illiteracy was widespread.

The Education Act of 1870 provided that School Boards must be set up if there was a proven deficiency in the educational system. These boards could build schools and were allowed to pass by-laws making it compulsory for children to attend school between the ages of five and thirteen.[1] The Act,

[1] For the full effects of the Act see Mary Sturt, *The Education of the People: A History of Primary Education in England and Wales in the Nineteenth Century*, Routledge and Kegan Paul, 1967, pp. 313–41.

Every year, farm workers hold a rally in the village of Tolpuddle. Their banners show that they are still among the lowest-paid workers, as they were a century ago

however, did not make education either efficient or compulsory overnight.

Education—as it too often has been—was provided on the cheap. Monitors, who had to be over twelve years of age and to have passed the Standard IV examination, were paid 1s or so a week to look after classes for up to three hours a day.[1] In practice, however, they often acted as teachers, because of shortages of staff.

Another extremely unsatisfactory aspect of the educational system were the pupil-teachers, who were often little older than the monitors: they were neither sufficiently instructed as pupils nor sufficiently qualified to teach. After working for thirty hours a week, they were expected to fit in their teacher-training from the headmaster or the headmistress before or after school or in the midday break. In 1870, the proportion of pupil-teachers to teachers was about half; by 1885, when some pupil-teacher training centres started to open in the large cities, it had been reduced to about 30 per cent.[2]

[1] Cf. Hugo Rice-Wiggin and Alfred Perceval Graves, *The Elementary School Manager*, London, 1879, p. 72.
[2] Cf. Sturt, op. cit., p. 365.

Part of the teachers' pay often came from the school fees of 2d or 3d a week, paid by parents who could ill afford them. Teachers were also paid by results. The government grant to schools, which sometimes contributed towards the teachers' salaries, was based primarily on the numbers of children who passed the yearly examination. The annual visit of the school inspector was a dreaded event.

Equipment was often rudimentary. One village school in 1867 received one dozen pieces of chalk, a bottle of ink and a dozen pencils for the year. In 1877, another school was still unprovided with desks, and there was no blackboard or easel.[1]

It was little wonder that many parents, especially those with large families, kept their children away from school. In 1876 an Act was passed making it the duty of parents to see that their children attended school, and four years later it was made compulsory for all children to go to school until the age of ten. But it was not until education was made free in 1891 that it became possible to ensure that children did attend regularly.

Even before that, however, the efforts of dedicated teachers in those appalling conditions and the concern of some parents to provide a better education for their children, had brought about some improvements in educational standards. These better-educated youths tended to move away from the villages when they grew up or later to cycle to employment in the nearest town. The effect of this rural exodus was that the villages became more and more the refuge of the middle-aged and the old, cut off from the mainstream of modern life, and denuded of their most youthful and ambitious inhabitants.

There were few really significant improvements in villages during the rest of the century. The state of cottages had always varied greatly, even in the same village. Most families lived in four-roomed cottages, like the Strudwicks. There were a fortunate few who lived in much more commodious cottages with three bedrooms, a living-room, a scullery, a bakehouse with an oven, and good outhouses in the large garden, which often also contained a pigsty.

Some of the biggest and wealthiest landowners had a fine record for providing good accommodation on their estates, particularly the seventh Duke of Bedford who started building model cottages after he succeeded to the title in 1839. (The Russell family have always had a great tradition of agricultural improvement, which extends back to the seventeenth century when the fourth Earl of Bedford (1593–1641) took the leading part in the draining of the Fens.) Between 1847 and 1867, the Dukes of Northumberland built or improved 931 cottages for workers on their estates. The seventh Earl of

---

[1] Cf. M. K. Ashby, *The Country School, Its Practice and Problems*, Oxford University Press, 1929, p. 71.

Shaftesbury, the social reformer, was another landlord who made great improvements on his family estates at Wimborne, Dorset. 'Every cottage', *The Times* noted, 'has its apricot tree, its pump, its separate sanitary arrangements, its pigsty, and its quarter-acre allotment—the labourer paying for all these things only 52s per annum.'[1]

In contrast, many of the absentee landowners, the squirearchy, and the speculators who owned village cottages, did little to improve their property.[2] Some of the worst accommodation was owned by the farm workers themselves: small, dilapidated, tumbledown cottages, consisting of one room with an earth floor. These primitive conditions persisted in some isolated parts of the country right up to the Second World War, and even beyond. Though there was some public concern about the wretched conditions in which farm workers lived, public attention was concentrated far more on the conditions in industrial towns.

The small, overcrowded, damp cottages, the impure water supplies, the lack of adequate sanitation, and the deficiencies in diet, all combined to lower the health of the rural population. The farm workers avoided some of the worst effects of their polluted environment by never drinking water but only weak tea or beer. Nevertheless, every village was more or less a fever bed.[3] Tuberculosis was common and there were frequent epidemics of measles and whooping cough which killed many children. The men benefited by working in the open air and by having the largest share of the available food, though most of them were afflicted by what they called rheumatism. The wives and the children, who were frequently undernourished, showed the deficiencies in their diet more clearly, the boys being stunted in growth, and many of the girls being taller and angular. Some of the country doctors gave good service to the farm workers and their families. But village people often relied on the advice of the local 'wise woman' in sickness and the help of neighbours in confinements.

From the available evidence, it would seem that wages rose slightly from the 1840s and were increased by a few shillings during the course of Joseph Arch's agitation. This upwards trend was checked during the agricultural depression, though there were some slight increases again in some places towards the end of the nineteenth century. But there was no general improvement. In 1892, the average income of one representative Somerset farm labourer was 11s 6½d a week. He had two boys of nine years and six months of age, and three girls of thirteen, seven and five living at home, another two daughters in domestic service, and a crippled son apprenticed to a boot-maker. His home, an old abandoned farmhouse, was rent-free, but too large

[1] *The Times*, 2 October 1885.
[2] Cf. Edward Smith, *The Peasant's Home, 1760–1875*, London, 1876, pp. 92–5.
[3] Cf. ibid., p. 9.

for him either to heat or furnish adequately. Their food consisted mainly of tea, bread, butter and potatoes, bacon at nearly every meal, vegetables, and a pudding for dinner. They never had fresh meat.[1] Indeed, the farm worker still remains one of the lowest-paid manual workers. According to an official sample survey, average earnings of all farm workers in England and Wales in 1969–70 were just over £18 for a 48-hour week.[2]

During the latter part of the nineteenth century the decreasing demand for farm labour, and other factors, brought about a decline in the number of women and children working on the land. Even by the early 1880s it was unusual in some districts to find women working regularly on farms; they were employed only for seasonal work such as fruit picking and potato lifting. For many years, women and young children from the age of six had been regularly employed in agricultural gangs in the eastern counties. Gangmasters hired them out to the highest bidder. In 1867 a law was passed forbidding the employment of children under eight in these gangs, and six years later another law made it illegal to employ children under eight on farms at all.

From the 1870s onwards there were increasingly rapid changes in the kind of work that men did on farms. In addition to using their traditional skills, they had to learn how to use new methods and new machinery. Although corn drills, mechanical reapers and threshing machines had all been invented at an earlier period, farm mechanization on any scale started only in the middle of the century. About that time a few farmers started using steam ploughs, but they never became very popular. Threshing by machine, however, was firmly established on some large farms by 1815. The first machines were driven by horse or water power, and by 1870 possibly 80 per cent of corn was being threshed mechanically, most of it by steam-powered machines. But there was no sudden transition from hand to machine methods, so that threshing by hand continued in some places into the 1930s and hand tools are still used for the harvest on some small farms in the north and west until this day.[3] In the same way, oxen had long been replaced by horses on most farms, but they continued to be used in parts of Sussex into the twentieth century, and there was still one herd of oxen at work in 1939.[4] These were exceptions. By the end of the century, horses were the main draught animals on farms and most corn

---

[1] Cf. Economic Club, *Family Budgets: Being the Income and Expenses of Twenty-Eight British Households, 1891–1894*, London, 1896, p. 48.
[2] Cf. *Land Worker*, Journal of the National Union of Agricultural and Allied Workers, London, May, 1971.
[3] Cf. E. J. T. Collins, *Sickle to Combine: A Review of Harvest Techniques from 1800 to the Present Day*, Museum of English Rural Life, University of Reading, 1969, pp. 7–8 and 35.
[4] Cf. H. J. Massingham, *Country Relics*, Cambridge University Press, 1939, pp. 100–1.

Ploughing by oxen still continued in a few parts of the country into the present century. The date of this photograph is about 1880

Steam ploughing engines, which had the plough attached to a long cable, never became very popular. This one was bought in 1864 by Mr Benjamin Bomford of Pitchill, Evesham, Worcestershire, who is sitting at the rear of the machine

was being cut mechanically by a reaping machine or by a self-binder which automatically tied the corn into sheaves. Tractors were used increasingly after the end of the First World War and combine harvesters after the Second World War.

Changes came just as slowly and spasmodically in village life. As the nineteenth century drew to its close, more cottages were fitted with kitchen grates with ovens in which meat could be roasted and bread could be baked; farm workers with sons and daughters working in nearby towns were better off and could afford to buy a few more possessions and to eat better food; candles were replaced increasingly by paraffin lamps and rushlights became a thing of the past. Some of the old village institutions, like the local benefit clubs, collapsed and were replaced by local branches of the national Manchester Unity of Oddfellows or the Ancient Order of Foresters—well-organized friendly societies which provided something more than an excuse for an annual dinner.

In other ways, however, life went on unchanged. Children still chanted the traditional rhyming games. In Derbyshire they said:

> Ink, pink, pen and ink
> I command for you to wink,
> Rottom, bottom, dish, clout,
> O.U.T. spells out,
> So out goes she.

In Cumberland, it went:

> Eeney, Pheeney, Figgery, Fegg,
> Deely Dyly ham and egg
> Calico back and stony rock
> Arlum, barlum, bash.[1]

Some of the older men continued to wear smocks into the twentieth century. Superstitions from a much earlier period of history still persisted. Until quite recently in West Sussex the thatcher attached to the last hay rick a straw dolly, which was intended originally not as decoration but as a tribute to a pagan god for the success of the harvest. Women put their shoes in the shape of a cross by their bed at night or carried the right fore-foot of a hare in their pocket in the hope that it would cure rheumatism.[2] A century ago, belief in witchcraft was still so strong in villages that a mother, who believed that a neighbour had bewitched her child, scratched the woman's arm with a crooked pin to see if any blood would come.[3]

Not all these beliefs are dead today. Some villagers continued to believe in witches into modern times. Many people everywhere think it is unlucky to look at a new moon through glass. Belief in the blackthorn winter still exists in West Sussex. Villagers still have a lively sense of their own rights, so that they refuse to give up using public footpaths, even if corn is grown on them, and still ignore notices prohibiting the picking of wild flowers in private woods. They retain a great sense of identity with the countryside and refer to 'our farm', even though they do not own it, and know the name of every field and of every cow they milk. They have a great sense of history, too, so that every year the National Union of Agricultural and Allied Workers holds a memorial rally in Tolpuddle, Dorset, to honour the 'martyrs' who were transported in 1834.

Although the motor-car and the television set have brought them more into the mainstream of modern life, they still retain more simple qualities from the

---

[1] Robert Charles Hope, 'Derbyshire and Cumberland Counting-Out and Children's Game Rhymes', *The Folk Lore Journal*, London, vol. 1, 1883.
[2] Charlotte Latham, 'Some West Sussex Superstitions Lingering in 1868', *The Folk Lore Record*, Part 1, London, n.d. (1878), pp. 23–4.
[3] Cf. ibid, pp. 38–9.

past: their fortitude and patience; their lively sense of justice and of humour; their belief in themselves and in the value of the work they do. These are the qualities which carried them through the long years of privation and gave them strength to bear their hard lot. It was in this sense alone that the picture of the happy countryman of the past was true.

Appendix 1
Changes in the Countryside

The following list of dates may be found useful for reference. It should be remembered that many years often elapsed between the invention of a machine and its widespread adoption by farmers. Similarly, Acts of Parliament did not always become immediately effective everywhere. For example, critics claimed that some of the provisions of the Agricultural Gangs Act of 1867 were still being evaded in the 1890s.

c. 1784	Andrew Meikle's threshing machine.
c. 1828	Patrick Bell's reaping machine.
1830	'Swing' riots.
1834	Six 'Tolpuddle Martyrs' sentenced to transportation.
1836	Tithe Commutation Act substituted a rent-charge for the tithe of one-tenth of the products of the farm.
1840s	Two national voluntary societies started to open schools in villages.
1846	Repeal of the Corn Laws, which eventually allowed cheap wheat to be imported from the New World.
1851	Great Exhibition in London stimulated farmers to buy machinery with its displays of English and American machinery.
1867	Agricultural Gangs Act prohibited children under eight years of age from working in gangs on the land.
1870	Education Act set up school boards to provide new schools wherever they were needed.
1872	Licensing Act prohibited playing games for money on licensed premises and restricted hours of opening.
1872	Joseph Arch formed National Agricultural Labourers' Union, which organized strikes in many parts of the country.
1873–4	Lock-outs in various places.
1873	Agricultural Children's Act banned all children under eight from working on farms.
1875	Sale of Food and Drugs Act instituted heavy fines for adulterating food.
c. 1875–95	Agricultural depression which had worst effects on corn producers and sheep farmers.
1878	Cyrus McCormick's self-binder.
1884	Representation of the People Act, the third reform bill, which gave country people the vote.
1891	Elementary education made free, though schools with higher fees could continue to make a weekly charge.

Appendix 2
Further Work

There are many different ways in which this material can be followed up. For example, some of the farm methods described in the narrative persisted into living memory and pupils might be encouraged to collect reminiscences from older people on the lines so successfully pioneered by George Ewart Evans. Examples of existing dialect might be tape-recorded. Photographs of old country scenes, and even some of the evictions following the 1873–4 lock-outs are still to be found in some country cottages. Many relics from this period still exist and these could be brought to school, sketched, photographed or described.

Even in urban areas equally profitable work on this subject may still be done. Street names often reveal the agricultural history of a place. Shepherds Hill might indicate that a shepherd's hut once stood in the fields which have now become the site of a densely packed estate of houses. (Old Ordnance Survey maps often provide the answer.) The transition to an urban economy in the last century could also be examined. The development or decline of local crafts and trades, such as basketry, thatching and milling, or of local institutions, such as schools, festivals, or friendly societies, are also worth studying. Two extremely useful bibliographies are: Andrew Jewell, *Crafts, Trades and Industries: A Book List for Local Historians*, National Council of Social Service, 1968; and F. G. Emmison, *English Local History Handlist: A Select Bibliography and List of Sources for the Study of Local History and Antiquities* (Helps for Students of History, No. 9), 4th edn, Historical Association, 1969.

There are a number of other useful sources for the study of local history. Most public libraries have local collections of books, pamphlets and other materials in which the history of the locality may be studied. Many local museums have objects relating to the agricultural past; there are a number of bigger regional collections; and there is the major centre for the collection of material on agricultural history at the Museum of English Rural Life, University of Reading. An increasing number of museums provide special services for schools, including loan services. What is generally available is helpfully described in Margaret E. Bryant's *The Museum and the School* (Teaching of History Leaflet, No. 6), Historical Association, 1961.

One source of material which is being increasingly used by a number of schools are local archives. Some university departments have produced local teaching history units. Many county and city archivists are encouraging schools to use their material by providing special facilities, conducted visits and photographic reproductions of documents.

Appendix 3
Further Reading

George Bourne, *Change in the Village*, Duckworth, 1st edn 1912, and subsequent editions.

Robert Douch, *Local History and the Teacher*, Routledge and Kegan Paul, 1967.

George Ewart Evans, *Ask the Fellows who Cut the Hay*, Faber, 1956.

J. Finberg, *Exploring Villages*, Routledge and Kegan Paul, 1958.

George Edwin Fussell, *The English Rural Labourer*, Batchworth Press, 1949.

William George Hoskins, *Fieldwork in Local History*, Faber, 1967.

Index

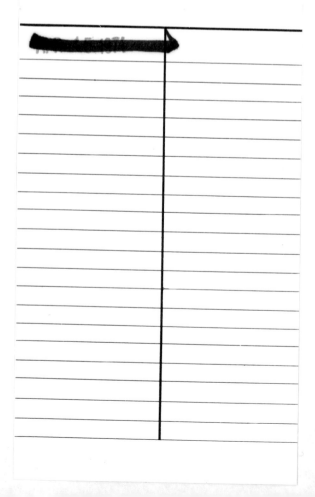

DATE DUE